"Doug Gladstone's compelling ... former major leaguers denied ... for generosity from those who surely can afford it. Owners pay multimillion dollar salaries to many young players today while, abetted by callous player union chiefs, they deny pittances of a few thousand dollars a year to many aging veterans trapped within a *Catch 22* of big league timing."

– Wayne Woodlief, Political columnist, *Boston Herald*

—◆—

"Become a major league baseball player, even for a single game, and you join one of the most exclusive fraternities ever. And today, with salaries ranging from the fantastic to the obscene, virtually none of the players who now qualify for the fabulous MLB pension plan should ever have to use it. So why can't the millionaire ballplayers and the billionaire owners find a way to take care of the few (and ever dwindling) number of former players who don't qualify for inclusion, yet so desperately need the help?

"While the players and owners certainly are within their legal rights to exclude these fellow athletes, that doesn't make it morally right, and Gladstone comes up clutch by exposing a sad, desperate, and shameful chapter of baseball's labor history."

– Mark Schraf, author of *Cooperstown Verses: Poems About Each Hall of Famer* and managing editor of *SPITBALL: The Literary Baseball Magazine*

"Mr. Gladstone does an excellent job of weaving these players' individual stories into a book that is also a social cause. He should be commended for continuing to look out for these men."

  – Edward F. Coyle, Executive Director of the Alliance for Retired Americans

—◆—

"Gladstone serves up far more than a 'bitter cup of coffee.' In fact, it's a must read for any baseball fan who really wants to understand baseball history, baseball finances, and just good old-fashioned modern day greed!"

  – David Sinow, J.D., Ph.D, Clinical Professor of Finance, University of Illinois at Urbana-Champaign

—◆—

"Doug Gladstone shines a much-needed light on an injustice that most fans aren't even aware of. Hopefully, *A Bitter Cup of Coffee* will finally spur the Players Association to act in favor of its forgotten constituents."

  – David H. Martinez, author of *The Book of Baseball Literacy*

A BITTER
Cup of Coffee

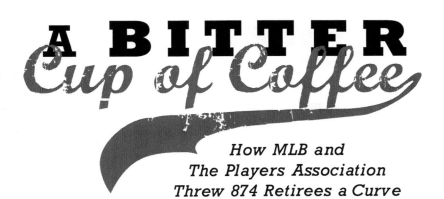

A BITTER Cup of Coffee

*How MLB and
The Players Association
Threw 874 Retirees a Curve*

Douglas J. Gladstone

WORD ASSOCIATION PUBLISHERS
www.wordassociation.com
1.800.827.7903

Printed in the United States of America.

ISBN: 978-1-59571-512-8

Library of Congress Control Number: 2010922241

Designed and published by

Word Association Publishers
205 Fifth Avenue
Tarentum, Pennsylvania 15084

www.wordassociation.com
1.800.827.7903

For my parents, Berdie and Joe, who gave me life.

And for my wife, Karen, and daughter, Jovie, who make my life worth living.

Thanks for

TABLE OF CONTENTS

FOREWORD

Do the right thing.

That's what Douglas J. Gladstone wants from Major League Baseball.

Extend the baseball family to include a small group of retired players in some form of retirement benefit, comparable to benefits awarded other former players whose careers left them ineligible for standard MLB pensions.

Not because MLB has to; Gladstone faces the fact that a court has ruled it doesn't, but because it is the right thing to do.

Just as it was the right and generous thing to award retirement benefits to some African-American ballplayers who couldn't, because of racist exclusion, play in the Big Leagues, Gladstone argues it would be right and generous to pony up some annuities for this small group of players who missed out on retirement benefits because they played in "the Bigs" for too short a time, at the exact wrong time.

And, if I may be so crass, stepping up to the plate here will silence a lot of wrong and hurtful things being said about Major League Baseball by angry petitioners, and, even in the pinched times at the end of the first decade of the 21ˢᵗ century, doing so is affordable.

This is all about 874 former players, all of them now at least middle-aged. None will ever play again, and every year, they are dying off, perpetually capping and shrinking the cost of their benefits, so settling something on "the short-timers" of 1947-1979 should contain no financial trapdoors for MLB and its players. This is a fix that will stay fixed.

The remarkable Basic Agreement negotiated between Major League Baseball and its players' union done in 1980 created a remarkable community: Everyone who played as much as a minute of big league baseball after 1980 is in the club, and is eligible for retirement benefits.

But what about the players whose brief contributions to the game occurred in those 33 seasons after Major Leaguers won some pension benefits and before the new Agreement? In the words of one owner, "They got screwed." They did not accrue the four years in the majors required for vesting before 1980, and did not play a minute after the fatal date. And, as of now, they are getting little or nothing from the game they loved.

Fixing this inadvertent injustice can be done, if both the owners and they players decide to do it. It will cost them marginal money to do so. They say they'll look at it in their next 2011 negotiation, but they should stop looking and start acting now. A simple side agreement could be executed anytime.

Doug Gladstone's *A Bitter Cup of Coffee* is a persuasive straightforward argument, a plea, really, for unscrewing the past, and laying a little hardball love on 874 small human contributors to what the Commissioner likes to call, "the world of Baseball." It is good reporting on a neglected topic, good thinking about potential solutions, and good writing about baseball reality.

Let me second Doug's emotion: Turn the replay machine on for this one, boys, and you'll see, a mistake has been made, and the fix is obvious: change the call.

Do the right thing.

ACKNOWLEDGEMENTS

I have been a fan of the national pastime ever since my late father took me to my first baseball game in 1967, when I was seven years old. Since then, I've listened to scores of games on the radio, seen countless games on television and been lucky enough actually to attend hundreds more at fields and stadiums across the country. The sport has been a constant in my life for most of the last four decades.

Growing up, I once read that baseball writers, and sports reporters in general, are usually fans of the games they cover. That's in marked contrast to other beat reporters. Obituary writers don't typically hang around funeral parlors, you know. Therefore, because I am, first and foremost, a fan of the game itself, this project was a labor of love for me.

Admittedly, I never really paid much attention to the business side of baseball. These days, of course, it's pretty hard to ignore that aspect of the sport. So, last June, when I was interviewing the former Chicago Cub, Jimmy Qualls, for a *Baseball*

Digest story that was ultimately published in September 2009, and he casually mentioned that he wasn't receiving a pension, being the inquisitive type, I asked him why. When he explained the reasons why he wasn't, I knew I had the makings of a story that had to be told.

Out of necessity, a journalist who writes a straight news story must always bring an unvarnished perspective to anything he or she writes. Well, as a proponent of advocacy journalism, I mention this because, in the interests of full disclosure, I want to be up front with everyone who reads this book. Since I personally believe these players have gotten the short end of the stick and been taken advantage of, I'm hoping that my work will help Qualls and all the men like him get their pensions.

I know my objectivity is going to be questioned. Naturally, people are going to believe what they want to believe. So, while I am confident my reporting, research and writing was responsible and honest, I'm willing to acknowledge the possibility that some people won't see it that way. To them, as well as all the readers of this book, I invite you to make up your own minds and judge for yourself whether I have presented a fair and balanced account.

Whether a reader believes the above statement or not, what is undeniable is that a lot of people willingly gave of their time to help me prepare this manuscript for publication. For starters, the wonderful folks at Word Association Publishers need to be singled out for their patience, counsel, advice and guidance. Dr. Tom Costello runs a great operation, and I am fortunate that he and his staff were so gracious in their interactions with me.

Next, to Gary Neibauer, it was always a pleasure visiting with you. This book couldn't have been written without your valuable contributions.

To all those other ballplayers whom I interviewed, I want you to know how indebted I am to you. So many of you often spent hours on the telephone with me, or took time out of your day to write thoughtful emails in response to my questions. In particular, I want to thank, in alphabetical order, Dick Baney, David Clyde, Steve Grilli, Jimmy Hutto, Eddie Robinson, Jim Sadowski, Craig Skok and Ken Wright.

I would also be remiss if I didn't acknowledge Rob Manfred and Pat Courtney, of Major League Baseball, for their forthrightness and professionalism.

For their invaluable support, I also want to thank attorney Jim Acho, accountant Ted Nocella and all those friends, family and colleagues at work who indulged me during the seven months it took to complete this manuscript.

To Dave Marash, given your accomplishments and reputation, I am honored and humbled that you agreed to write the foreword to my book. This time, the bagel and *schmear* are on me.

On occasion, I often wanted to quit this project and throw my hands up in disgust. Whenever that occurred, I remembered the words of Pamela "Nan" Grottanelli, whose dear husband, Rick, died while this book was being written. "I know Rick would greatly appreciate what you are doing," she wrote me in an email several weeks after he passed away. To her and her daughter, Serafina, I would say only this: besides my late parents, if an angel in heaven is looking over my shoulder, I hope it's Rick because, in the brief time that our paths crossed, he was someone whose generosity of spirit I admired greatly.

To my beautiful daughter, Jovie, I want you to know that I took up writing again after a protracted time away from my chosen field because of you. (Your mother will tell you it was because of my own ego and, while that may be somewhat true, it doesn't paint a complete picture!) I want you to know that you can aspire to be anything you want to be and accomplish anything you want to do in this life, even if the path you take is somewhat circuitous, like mine was. Remember not to let anyone ever tell you that you should put your dreams on hold.

Last, to my best friend, chief cheerleader and severest critic, my devoted wife, Karen, you have been my partner and hand holder from the get-go, so your blessings and encouragement meant everything to me. I love the life we've made for ourselves, and I will always love you and our daughter, forever and ever, which is a very long time.

First

INTRODUCTION

Since 1876, when the National League was founded, up until the start of the 2009 season, some 17,000 men have played the game of baseball.[1]

This is the sad story of 874 of those players, all of whom played between the years 1947 and 1979, and each had careers in the major leagues that are typically referred to as "cups of coffee."

According to the National Baseball Hall of Fame and Museum in Cooperstown, New York, the long defunct newspaper, *The New York Globe*, first used the term in its June 11, 1908 account of a game played the previous afternoon.[2] To have a cup of coffee, explains the *Dickson Baseball Dictionary*, means "a brief trial in the Major Leagues by a minor league player"; these trials normally take place in September, when major league rosters are expanded to 40 players. The phrase, the dictionary continues, "seems to have been derived from the observation that a young player's first taste

---

[1] Freddy Berowski, National Baseball Hall of Fame & Museum, A. Bartlett Giamatti Research Library, July 20, 2009.

[2] Berowski, National Baseball Hall of Fame & Museum, A. Bartlett Giamatti Research Library, July 17, 2009

of the majors is usually quite short, figuratively just long enough to drink a cup of coffee."[3]

The average career of a Major League Baseball player is 5.6 years, according to a 2007 study by a University of Colorado at Boulder research team. The study, which also found that one in five position players will have only a single-year career, and that at every point of a player's career, the player's chance of ending his career is at least 11 percent, examined the career statistics of baseball players who started their careers between 1902 and 1993. Pitchers were excluded because they were not everyday players. All told, the study revealed that, between 1902 and 1993, 5,989 position players started their careers and played 33,272 person years of Major League Baseball.[4]

The fact that none of these 874 players even remotely averaged 5.6 years in the major leagues is almost a moot point. Each of their respective cups of coffee was for varying lengths. Take Jimmy Qualls, for example. Best remembered for ruining Hall of Fame pitcher Tom Seaver's bid for a perfect game on July 9, 1969, when he singled with one out in the top of the ninth inning, over the course of three seasons, the former Chicago Cub played in a total of 63 games.

So just why is the length of a baseball player's career important? Because, together with salary earned, his service credit helps determine whether he's eligible to receive a pension from Major League Baseball (MLB).

[3] Paul Dickson, *The New Dickson Baseball Dictionary*, 3rd edition, March 2009 (W.W. Norton & Company).
[4] William Witnauer, Richard Rogers and Jarron Saint Onge, "Major League Baseball Career Length in the 20th Century," *Popular Research and Policy Review*, August 2007, University of Colorado at Boulder.

A pension from MLB is the gold standard among the four major professional sports leagues. "Modern-day players really should have nothing to worry about [financially]," said John Westhoff, baseball's onetime associate counsel. "The pension plan should take care of their finances in their older years."[5]

And that's why the stories of these men are so sad. As a result of a threatened players strike in 1980, the vesting requirments to earn a pension from MLB suddenly changed. Previously, the vesting requirement was four years. Since 1980, however, all a player has needed is one day of service credit for health benefits and 43 days of service credit to be eligible for a retirement allowance. Talk about a sweetheart deal!

Actually, it's the very opposite of sweet. Sour would be more like it. One might even suggest that these men gulped bitter cups of coffee.

Inexplicably, as part of the agreement which the Major League Baseball Players Association (MLBPA) ratified, once the '80 strike was called off, all those former ballplayers who played during the 1947-1979 seasons were not included retroactively in the amended vesting requirement.

"Did you know that more than 1,000 former big-leaguers don't receive a baseball pension—and are ineligible for medical coverage—only because they had the misfortune to conclude their careers before the players association bargained for a more inclusive retirement plan in 1980?" was the way one columnist started his story about the issue.[6]

---

[5] David Schwartz, "Baseball Pension Plan Tops in Pro Sports," *Street & Smith's Sports Business Journal*, March 1, 1999.
[6] John McGrath, "Baseball Wrong In Denying Pensions To Older Players," *Tacoma Times Record News*, May 10, 2004.

To be exact, when the aforementioned story was written, in 2004, there were 1,053 men who were affected by the vesting requirement change brokered during the 1980 strike talks. That was down from four years earlier, in February 2000, when there were approximately 1,400 men, according to Al Autry, the former Atlanta Braves hurler whose claim to baseball fame is that he is the only major league pitcher after World War II whose one start in the big leagues—he pitched five innings against the Houston Astros at Fulton County Stadium and gave up four hits while striking out three batters—was his *only appearance* in the big leagues.

Not that the union was required to do anything for these onetime ballplayers. Under the National Labor Relations Act, the association did not owe them a "duty of fair representation," says Lawrence W. Boes, a retired partner with the international law firm of Fulbright & Jaworski, LLP.

"When an employer argues that funding the pension system and that including already 'retired' employees adds tremendously to current labor costs, a union and its current members may be ready to abandon any consideration of former players who are not part of the collective bargaining unit and who are without voting rights in the union's processes of collective bargaining," explains Boes. "This may sound cynical, but it's a reality."[7]

Boes knows what he is talking about; over the course of his career, he litigated intellectual property and antitrust law cases in federal and state courts at both the trial and appellate levels, as well as representing a sports concessionaire at various MLB ballparks.

Realistically, under the union's previous Collective Bargaining Agreements (CBAs) with the league, those who were

---

[7] Lawrence W. Boes, email to author, July 19, 2009.

affected by the decision had no expectation they were ever going to get a pension in the first place. If you didn't have four years service credit, you weren't eligible. Period. End of discussion.

"[A pension] wasn't mine to have to begin with," agrees Qualls.[8]

However, in 1997, something occurred that changed the entire dynamics of this issue. At MLB's meeting in Scottsdale, Arizona, the executive council created a pension plan for about 85 black players who didn't play in the majors long enough to qualify for a pension or who did not have the opportunity to play in the majors at all.

Later that same year, the council also gave pensions to a group of non-black players who retired before 1947, the year the pension plan began.

Strictly speaking, these so called pensions weren't *really* pensions. Even MLB acknowledged the distinction. "Baseball is very proud of its support of Major League Baseball players and other members of the baseball family," said Rich Levin, the spokesman for the league in 2000. "In 1997, the major league baseball clubs established two separate supplemental benefit plans to assist former players. To date, over $2,000,000 has been paid to former players under these two benefit plans. One hundred and ninety-seven former players are currently receiving benefits under these plans and another twenty-seven have received benefits in the past."[9]

Make no mistake, many employers do offer supplemental benefit plans but, as that term implies, they supplement something else. What these players got was more akin to a life annuity, which

---

[8] Jimmy Qualls, phone interview with author, June 7, 2009.
[9] Bill Swank, "Strike Out," *The National Pastime*, January 1, 2000.

is a predetermined payout amount until the death of the annui-
tant. And these payments didn't include survivor benefits or health
insurance, which pensions typically provide.

To be eligible, the black players had to either play in the
Negro Leagues for at least one season before 1948 or play a
combined four years in the Negro Leagues and the major leagues
before 1979.[10]

Of course, African Americans had been unofficially barred
from the game until 1947, the year Jackie Robinson broke the color
barrier. Now, after years of both overtly and covertly discriminating
against black ballplayers, MLB was attempting to change its evil ways.
And really, who would argue with the rationale for doing so? Long
before that historic evening in November 2008, when this country
elected its first African-American president, baseball had too often
mirrored society's segregationist attitudes about race relations.

The price tag associated with this magnanimous gesture?
Annual payments of between $7,500 and $10,000 per player.

Baseball's then chief labor executive, Randy Levine, justified
the disbursement of the monies by noting that "Baseball wants to
take care of those who contributed so much to its past as it grows
in the future."[11]

That future got even brighter for the veterans of the Negro
Leagues in 2004, when Baseball Commissioner Allan "Bud" Selig
agreed to pay pensions to more of these ballplayers on the grounds
that baseball had not been totally integrated until 1959, when

---

[10] Murray Chass, "Pioneer Black Players To Be Granted Pensions," *The New York Times*, January 20,
1997.
[11] Ibid.

the Boston Red Sox became the last team to field a black player, Pumpsie Green.[12]

"This is an important step toward solving a terrible inequity," said United States Senator Bill Nelson, a Florida Democrat who successfully lobbied Selig about the supposed narrowness of the 1997 requirements. "These are some guys who really need and deserve help."[13]

The terms of the agreement weren't exactly the same as with the 1997 group of ex-Negro Leaguers. Players who never played in the major leagues were given the option of electing to choose pensions totaling $375 per month ($4,500 a year) for life or $10,000 a year for four years.[14]

But MLB wasn't finished atoning for its sins. As recently as 2008, baseball gave $5,000 payments to 30 former Negro League players who were matched with each of its teams. Acting on an idea from Hall of Famer Dave Winfield, who envisioned rewarding the old-timers with the equivalent of draft signing bonuses, each major league club selected one of the former ballplayers to honor at a ceremony in Florida, including Walter McCoy, who was selected by the San Diego Padres, and Neale "Bobo" Henderson, who was picked by the Los Angeles Angels of Anaheim.[15]

"We're gonna give 'em some money, give 'em some love and interview a lot of the people for posterity," said Winfield at the time. "They set the stage for major league baseball, to show that diversity works."[16]

---

[12] Gregory Lewis, "Selig Expected To Settle Dispute Over Negro League Pensions," *South Florida Sun Sentinel*, March 10, 2004.

[13] Michael O'Keefe, "Pensions to Reach More Negro Leaguers," *New York Daily News*, March 11, 2004.

[14] Doug Pappas, *Doug's Business of Baseball WebBlog*, May 16, 2004.

[15] Tim Sullivan, "The Real McCoy, Other Negro Leaguers Get Their Own Day in the Sun," *San Diego Union Tribune*, June 1, 2008.

[16] Ibid.

In attempting to help the former Negro League players, one might suggest that MLB had become the equivalent of the circus contortionist, bending over backwards, forwards, sideways and every which way but loose to ensure that past wrongs had been righted. However, while the lords of baseball had no problem doing the right thing for these African-American ballplayers, they showed absolutely no similar inclination to help the pre-1980, non-vested players.

Take Carmen Fanzone for instance. A third baseman for the Cubs during the 1970s, Fanzone was cut by the team just a few weeks short of the four years he needed to vest.

"It used to eat me to death thinking about it," said Fanzone. "After I got cut, I called every club, but got no answer. Then I broke my ankle and couldn't come back."[17]

The fact that the vast majority of these pre-1980, non-vested players were white made the failure to include them retroactively in the amended vesting requirement more than just a little ironic. All the more puzzling is the mission statement of the players association itself.

"The strength of the Association can be measured in its gains, and despite work stoppages of various lengths during eight CBA negotiations, the solidarity and resolve of the players has never been stronger," reads the statement, which can be found on the MLBPA's own website. "Each generation of players has passed along a legacy and a responsibility to the next generation—a legacy built on equality, loyalty and fair play."

---

[17] Greg Johnson, "Systems of Checks and Imbalances," *Los Angeles Times*, February 27, 2007.

"What's right is right. If they (the African American ball-players) deserve it, we deserve it," says Qualls. "If we had a little bit of compensation, it'd make our lives a lot easier."

Fact is, more than a decade ago, at least one owner apparently thought that these white ballplayers were also getting short-changed. According to a published account, when asked about MLB's decision to award pensions to the former Negro League players, Jerry Reinsdorf, the owner of the Chicago White Sox, blamed the union for dragging its heels.

"This is something that I've been bringing up for a long time," he said in 1997. "Of course, the union has always said no. Every time the union has been approached about this, they've been very negative."[18]

The old four-year service credit requirement, he continued, was one that the former Negro League players couldn't possibly hope to satisfy. "I got to thinking about how ridiculous it is," he said. "There are so few of these guys and they really did get screwed. Not just the Black guys, the white guys, too."[19]

"That was our smoking gun," says Mike Colbern, the former Chicago White Sox catcher whose play earned him a spot on *Baseball Digest's* All-Rookie Team in 1978. "That's why we went to court."[20]

Believing that they were the victims of racial discrimination, as a result of the favorable treatment accorded the Negro League veterans, Colbern, former New York Met infielder Al Moran and Ernie Fazio, the first player ever signed by the expansion Houston Colt .45s—the team name was later changed to the

[18] "Negro Leaguers Get Pensions," *New Pittsburgh Courier*, February 1, 1997.
[19] Ibid.
[20] Michael Colbern, email to author, July 26, 2009.

Astros—were the lead plaintiffs in a class action lawsuit filed in October 2003 against MLB that alleged that their Title VII rights had been violated. Title VII of the Civil Rights Act of 1964 specifically prohibits employment discrimination based on race, color, religion, sex, or national origin.

In addition, the suit contended that team owners conspired to fund the pension benefits for the former Negro Leaguers, knowing that the white players who had played similar lengths of time in the big leagues had not received the same benefits.[21]

The suit also charged the team owners with gross negligence, suggesting that major league team doctors between 1947 and 1979 knew that giving players repeated injections of the legal drug cortisone was risky but that, in spite of such knowledge, the ballplayers were never warned of the potential long-lasting consequences to their health.[22]

Colbern says that MLB doctors gave the players illegal drugs, as well.

"Baseball gave us illegal drugs and too many cortisone shots but never kept medical records in order to keep us playing," he says. "I was actually given a drug, *Butazolidin,* which at the time had been taken off the market for human use in 1970."

A non-steroidal anti-inflammatory drug, Butazolidin made headlines in 1960 when it was rumored that the winner of the Kentucky Derby that year, a thoroughbred named Venetian Way, got a serious leg up on its competition when the drug was administered to the horse by its trainer.[23]

[21] "Lawsuit Alleges Discrimination Due to Race," *The Associated Press,* October 17, 2003.
[22] Dave Anderson, "Remembering Players M.L.B. Has Forgotten," *New York Times,* March 13, 2004.
[23] William Leggett, "The Mysterious Buty Treatment," *Sports Illustrated,* August 1, 1960.

"I had massive gastritis and duodenitis and was hospitalized for four days in Wichita, Kansas," recalls Colbern. "The trainer never said it was because of the bute that I was given."

Though he found the players' case "sympathetic," U.S. District Judge Manuel Real in March 2004 ultimately granted MLB's motion for a summary judgment, agreeing with the Commissioner's Office that the payments for the former Negro players "were not tied to any MLB employment relationship, rather, they were conferred as charitable donations." The league also said the players waited too long to raise any legal objections.[24]

Not surprisingly, the players appealed Real's ruling and, on December 6, 2005, the Ninth U.S. Circuit Court in California heard oral arguments from both sides. Less than six months later, on May 22, 2006, the court of appeals for the ninth circuit upheld the lower court's decision.

Writing for the three-judge panel, Justice Stephen Reinhardt indicated that the players had failed to establish a *prima facie* case of discrimination, given that the enactment of the Negro League Plans did not constitute an adverse employment action and given that the two groups of players are not similarly situated.[25]

"Even if appellants had made such a *prima facie* showing, we would conclude that Major League Baseball has provided a legitimate, non-discriminatory and non-pretextual reason for their decision to implement the plans," he continued. "The plans were adopted for the specific purpose of providing benefits to those who

---

[24] Michael R. Blood, "Former Baseball Players Lose Bid For Pensions, Benefits," *The Associated Press*, March 16, 2004.

[25] Kenneth Otgang, "Ninth Circuit Rejects Former Ballplayers' Suit on Pensions," *Metropolitan News Enterprise*, May 10, 2006.

had been discriminated against by being denied the opportunity to play MLB and to qualify for MLB benefits."[26]

Three years later, the lawyer for the players, Jason L. Rumsey, a senior associate with the Woodland Hills, California firm of DaCorsi, Placencio & Rumsey, P.C., is still troubled by MLB's failure to take care of the members of the class-action suit. "It is unfortunate," he said in June 2009. What is especially sad, he added, is that, in the intervening years since the appellate court's ruling, so many of the players had passed away.

As of October 18-24, 2009, which the United States Congress had declared as "National Save for Retirement Week," only 874 of the 1,053 players named in the class-action lawsuit were still alive.

Of course, both MLB and the MLBPA could address the matter, if they wanted to. And there is certainly precedent to do so. During All-Star weekend in 2007, the National Basketball Association (NBA) and the union representing its current ballplayers announced with great fanfare that the "Pre-65ers"—those pro-basketball players with three or four years of NBA service who played in the 1950s—would receive a 50 percent increase in their annuity, from $2,400 to $3,600 annually per year of service. Significantly, the vesting eligibility requirement to receive a pension was also lowered from five years to three years, the same as for those players who play now.[27]

When the current collective bargaining agreement between the MLBPA and MLB runs out in 2011, however, the thorny issue of the pre-1980, non-vested ballplayer is not expected to be an action

[26] Ibid.
[27] Ron Kroichick, "Pensions in Pro Sports; An Age-Old Issue for all the Big Leagues," *San Francisco Chronicle*, March 18, 2007.

item; instead, an overhaul of the MLB amateur draft is supposedly what is most important to the players association.

According to one account, the union may agree to a negotiated system of draft bonuses on a descending scale that is similar to what the NBA has.[28] That way, smaller market teams would have the ability to sign quality players, rather than be able only to select players they know they can sign.

As egregious as MLB's actions have been, one can argue that the players union, whose pension fund has been described as the most well-funded in American labor, and which was ironically not named as a defendant in the class-action suit, is just as culpable in this matter.[29] Indeed, some baseball executives feel that, had the verdict in the class-action suit not gone in MLB's favor, then the union should have been responsible for paying the judgment the players would be entitled to.[30]

What exactly might it cost to give these men and/or their survivors a pension? Gary Neibauer, the former relief pitcher for the Atlanta Braves and Philadelphia Phillies, who serves on a special pension benefits committee of the Major League Baseball Players Alumni Association (MLBPAA), formed to investigate ways to do just that, believes it would be a drop in the bucket.

Even if they only received the same $10,000 benefit allowance the former Negro Leaguers are getting each year, Neibauer reasons that would be better than the current state of affairs.

And it's not like MLB is going broke anytime soon. Commenting about the labor peace the game has enjoyed with the union since 2002, which was the last time the players entertained

[28] Buster Olney, "System Failure," *ESPN The Magazine*, July 27, 2009.
[29] Anderson, "Remembering Players M.L.B. Has Forgotten," *New York Times*, March 13, 2004.
[30] Ibid.

the notion of going out on strike, Rob Manfred, executive vice president for labor relations and human resources, said that baseball "has grown from $3.4 billion in revenue to more than $6 billion" since then.[31]

"The value of peace exceeds anything we might be fighting over," continued Manfred, "and the benefit of not having a stoppage far outweighs anything either side might gain."[32]

In striving for harmonious relations with today's ballplayers, however, MLB has actually done a profound disservice to old-timers such as Qualls and Fanzone. For, just as the former Negro Leaguers and pre-1947 players made contributions to the game, so too did the men in the class-action lawsuit.

Practically, even if MLB and the players association suddenly announced with much fanfare that they were prepared to give all the affected ballplayers and/or their beneficiaries pensions, Jim Sadowski, a member of the board of directors of the MLBPAA, doesn't think either would be able to. A vice president and financial advisor with Hefren-Tillotson, Inc., Sadowski posted a 0-1 record with one strikeout pitching in four games in 1974 for the Pittsburgh Pirates. His service credit in the big leagues totaled all of 27 days.

Often referring to himself as "the fourth Sadowski"—his uncles Ed, Ted and Bob all played in the big leagues, as well— Sadowski the banker said in the summer of 2009 that, with the economy in a downturn, and with the union not getting good rates of returns on its investments, both MLB and the players association may actually be able to fall back on the old chestnut

---

[31] Craig Muder, "Peace and Prosperity," *Memories And Dreams*, Spring 2009, Volume 31, Number 2, p. 9, The National Baseball Hall of Fame and Museum.
[32] Ibid.

that the time isn't right to fund new pensions because of Wall Street's problems.

"I've seen the financials the union and MLB show us," added Sadowski. "It's not a rosy picture."

Craig Skok serves with Neibauer on the same alumni committee that's trying to figure out ways to get these men their pensions. Though he already receives a benefit allowance from MLB, when informed of Sadowski's gloom and doom pronouncement, he volunteers that his "own pension has decreased by 22 percent."

In his review of *Field of Dreams*, Roger Ebert, the nationally renowned film critic, writes that the movie resonated with audiences chiefly because its creators "love baseball, and they think it stands for an earlier, simpler time when professional sports were still games and not industries."[33]

In this case, taking a step into the past has proven to be not so simple.

---

[33] Roger Ebert, *Chicago Sun Times*, April 21, 1989.

CHAPTER 1

In "Goodbye, Farewell and Amen," the final episode of the iconic classic, *M*A*S*H*, the pompous doctor portrayed by actor David Ogden Stiers, "Major Charles Emerson Winchester," gets a sendoff that's arguably one of the most indelible images in television history. After seven seasons of Winchester trumpeting his own self-importance, sophistication, breeding and surgical skills, like a proud peacock strutting his feathers, this upper-crust scion of a prominent Boston family leaves Korea on a garbage truck.

Such irony is not lost on Fazio, the former Colt .45 bonus baby who believes he and the other pre-1980, non-vested players are now part of baseball's garbage heap. A resident of the City of Alamo, where he lives only one block from his friend and neighbor, St. Louis Cardinals manager Tony LaRussa, Fazio, who actually does work as a manager at a sanitation company in Hayward, California, and who has spent the better part of the last three decades working in the refuse business for various companies, once sat atop the baseball world. Now, he feels just like disposable garbage. For, like someone taking out the trash, Fazio thinks he has been unfairly tossed out of the game.

The quintessential good glove / no stick type of player, Fazio's lifetime batting average over 141 games with the Colts / Astros and Kansas City A's was only .182. However, despite not being much of a hitter, one would never characterize Fazio as being a lightweight. You don't take on MLB in court if you don't possess the courage of your convictions.

"Baseball did not back us up," he says. "We deserve that pension. And that's what bothers me now."

"I am always getting calls from the widows of the guys, or the players themselves," continues Fazio, who did community relations work in the 1970s for Charley Finley's Oakland Athletics after his playing career ended. "They're always asking what went wrong. And I don't know what to tell them."

Consequently, nobody would begrudge Fazio if he asked what's going on. To help answer the question, we could ask Lem Barney, the former Detroit Lions cornerback who was inducted into the Pro Football Hall of Fame, in Canton, Ohio, in 1992.

Besides having sung background vocals on the classic Marvin Gaye song of the same name, Barney is actively involved in the movement to improve pensions paid to retired National Football League players.[34]

Now an ordained minister, Barney, whose godson, Jim Acho, is Fazio's attorney, is a member of the Gridiron Greats Assistance Fund, a nonprofit group that provides financial assistance and medical care to retired football players in need.

---

[34] Clifton Brown, "Ex-Players Say Increase in Pensions Is Needed," *New York Times*, February 2, 2007.

"Out of the four professional sports—baseball, football, basketball and hockey—we have the worst pension and we have a larger fraternity of men than the other three leagues put together," said Barney in an online interview in May 2009. "But the injuries are more severe, the head injuries are more damaging. It's been studied and shown that Alzheimer's, dementia and Parkinson's come from a lot of head-on collisions and head banging, and still they have not done anything to adjust it."

"I think owners should be a little more compassionate in that way," he continued, "but still nothing else has happened with that, so there's nothing I can do, just keep praying that sometime, someday that they will see that they need to look at that. They're still giving all the money to the rookies, millions of dollars. Maybe they should throw some of that in the pot for a lot of the former ballplayers who are suffering now."[35]

Maybe they should at that. The ballplayers, after all, are the ones who we pass through the turnstiles to see—not the owners in their luxury boxes. "The athletes are the only people in sports who count, they're the only ones who are indispensable," said that keen observer of the human condition, the late comedian, George Carlin. "Everyone else is superfluous."[36]

Helping his baseball brethren is certainly the reason that Moran agreed to attach his name like flypaper to the class-action suit. In part, that's because he attended a private parochial school, Detroit Catholic Central High School, which seeks to prepare its graduates to become productive members of society. Central's motto? "Teach Me Goodness, Discipline and Knowledge."

---

[35] Michael Shelton, "The Lem Barney Interview," *Spinal Column Newsweekly,* May 20, 2009.
[36] George Carlin, "Sports Roundup," *Brain Droppings*, Hyperion Books, 1997, p. 59.

"I didn't get on board to help myself," agreed Moran in July 2009.

A career .195 hitter who got 64 hits in 331 at-bats for the Mets in 1963, when his playing days came to an end, Moran, who up until recently worked for a construction company, eventually returned to his alma mater, where he coached the baseball team for 25 years. Future Reds third baseman Chris Sabo was among his disciples.

"I didn't give a crap about myself," continued Moran, "because frankly, I've done alright for myself. But I was worried about all the guys who really needed the help."

Guys like Sadowski's late uncle, Ted, for example. Moran says that Ted's brother, Bob, a pitcher during the 1960s for the Milwaukee Braves and the Boston Red Sox, contacted him nearly 30 years later to advise him that his brother, a middle-reliever who had played for the Senators and Twins during the same decade, was battling cancer. Moran says Bob Sadowski told him that, in spite of numerous appeals for assistance, MLB wasn't lifting a finger to help Ted, who finally succumbed to his illness on July 18, 1993.

Less than five months later, on November 6, 1993, tragedy struck the Sadowski clan again, when amyotrophic lateral sclerosis (ALS), often referred to as "Lou Gehrig's Disease," claimed the life of Ed Sadowski, who had been Joe Torre's backup catcher while with the Atlanta Braves and who would later serve as a pitching coach for the Montreal Expos.

Sadowski, who proudly acknowledges that "the game of baseball allowed me to open lots of doors for myself," and who specializes in providing in-depth financial planning and money management services for small- to medium-sized businesses, business executives, school teachers, retirees and professional athletes, says he is now "obsessed" with getting his uncle, Bob, the only one of the three brothers who is still alive, a pension.

A resident of Sharpsburg, Georgia, Bob Sadowski is a self-described member of baseball's old guard. "I'm not a baseball fan anymore," he tells a caller. "Not because I'm not getting a pension, but because the players are different these days."

Asked to elaborate, the 71-year-old former hurler, who compiled a won-loss record of 20-27 and an Earned Run Average (ERA) of 3.87 over his career, says that, when he played, he was happy to sign bubble gum cards for free. Today's players, he points out, command "ridiculous amounts of money for their autographs."

"Was I really going to charge someone for my signature?" he asks. "Was I going to force some mother or father to tell their son or daughter that they couldn't afford my price? Of course not. I was upholding the goodness of the game, and I didn't need to be paid for that."

One time, Sadowski says he even returned a $10 check to a father in Evanston, Illinois who was seeking his signature for his son. "I looked this fellow up in the phone book and called the guy and he couldn't believe it," he says, proudly. "He said, 'Mr. Sadowski, what an honor.' And I said, 'Mister, I'm the one who should be honored that you thought so much of me to want my autograph for your boy. That's payment enough for me.' And he says, 'But I already sent you a check.' And I told him I had already sent it back."

"It was the same when we went to senior citizen homes or children's hospitals," Sadowski continues. "I didn't get paid for doing those things, I did them because I was promoting baseball and it was the right thing to do."

Asked if giving a pension to men such as himself is the right thing to do, Sadowski diplomatically answers that it's not for him to say. However, he does volunteer that, given his assorted list of ailments, he could always use some more money to help defray expenses.

Time has not been good to the 6 foot 4 inch right-hander, whose wife passed away 25 years ago. He adds that, shortly after his loss, he suffered kidney failure. "I was on a dialysis machine, but I didn't like being hooked up to it," he recalls. "Fortunately, one day I woke up and my appetite returned. The doctors said it was a miracle."

A year later, Sadowski says he suffered a stroke that not only impacted his speech—he is still apt to slur his words—but also limited the mobility in his right arm and legs. Because he says he is also arthritic, he subsequently underwent two knee operations.

Sadowski says he is sometimes prone to feeling sorry for himself, and concedes he doesn't know where he'd be if it weren't for his fiancée, who has acted as his primary caregiver for years. "I realize I'm never going to be the way I was before, when I was in my prime," he says. "But I'm a hard-headed guy, and I had a heck of a career. If we get any money, that would help me out a lot."

Guys like Kenneth Wright could also benefit from a pension. Originally signed by the Boston Red Sox as a free agent in the 1964 amateur draft, Wright debuted with the Kansas City Royals in April 1970. With a won-loss record of 11-15 and a 4.54 ERA under his belt, the right-handed hurler ended his career almost four years later as a member of the New York Yankees.

Nearly three decades later, at the age of 63, Wright could be found working two jobs just to make ends meet. A courier for a local hospital, the Pensacola, Florida resident has also for the past 15 years managed the Warrington Emergency Aid Center, which distributes food and clothing for the needy.

Though his plight isn't as bad as those he serves on a daily basis, Wright admits he needs a pension just the same. Afflicted with type 2 diabetes, Wright says he suffers from diabetic ulcers on his feet.

Consequently, when Wright on June 5, 2008 wrote a letter to Commissioner Selig, in which he asked for information about whether or not he and the other non-vested players would ever receive pension benefits, it wasn't Selig who replied to him, but rather Manfred.

"As you are probably aware," the baseball executive indicated in his June 30, 2008 response to Wright, "player pensions are a subject of collective bargaining with the MLBPA. While, at various times, there have been conversations about pensions benefits for non-vested players, those conversations have not progressed to the point that I could even attempt to respond with any specificity to your inquiries. In fact, you should not make any decision, financial or otherwise, based on the assumption that benefits will be forthcoming from the Major League Baseball Players Benefit Plan."

Almost one year later, Manfred's words were different, but his message was still the same. In a statement sent to the author by his aide, Pat Courtney, Manfred stressed that "with every pension plan there are employees who fall short of the required service. Plans are funded on the assumption those rules will continue to be enforced. All of our plans—the Players Plan, the pre-1947 plan and the Negro League Plan—apply a four-year service requirement."[37]

Manfred's words bothered not only Wright, but his good friend and fellow Pensacola resident, Jimmy Hutto, as well. A catcher who debuted with the Philadelphia Phillies on April 17, 1970, when he was just 22 years old, Hutto played in 57 games that season, had 17 hits in 92 at bats, including three home runs and two doubles, and drove in 12 runs.

Five years later, the University of Southern Mississippi graduate was trying to hang on with the Baltimore Orioles. Though he got into four games with Baltimore in 1975, that's not what Hutto remembers about his time with the Birds.

"The Orioles treated me wonderfully during spring training in 1971," he recalls. "My wife miscarried, but the many flowers and cards sent to her then went a long way towards her recovery."

In an October 7, 2008 letter to Hall of Famer Brooks Robinson, one of the stars of those Oriole squads in the early 1970s, Hutto reminded the player once called the "Human Vacuum Cleaner," because of his fielding prowess at third base, of the kindness he felt for Robinson and the Orioles. "I know that you had a lot to do with it personally," Hutto wrote Robinson, referring to the trinkets his wife received, "and I thank you so much. That's the way we treated each other and our families back in that era."

Unfortunately, the passage of time had soured Hutto on the good feelings that had been engendered nearly three decades earlier. Seems that, in his official capacity as president of the board of the alumni association, Robinson had written Hutto requesting he renew his member dues.

---

[37] June 25, 2009 email to the author.

Bereft of a pension, Hutto responded to the solicitation by giving Robinson a piece of his mind. "Has the MLBPAA done anything toward bringing me and the other 900 or so (pre-1980, non-vested) players closer to receiving the same benefits for our time served as today's player or even the former Negro League players?

"We have sued in federal court and we have appealed in federal court," continued Hutto. "But no one has come forward to help right this wrong… where does the buck stop and when does someone stand up for us?"

If he hadn't made his point clearly before, Hutto then framed the debate in as concise a manner as he could. "Shouldn't the MLBPAA take the bull by the horns and really do some representing?" he asked Robinson.

"I am crippled with arthritis brought on by the abuse I put my body through playing baseball," continued Hutto, whom Wright says is too proud to reveal that he's also had an aneurysm that's left him with short term memory loss. "I am permanently disabled physically, but my brain is still working. And it's telling me that no one in baseball has the balls to do what is right and put our group of 900 guys on the same level playing field with all those other guys who are receiving benefits.

"I am just a regular person who played baseball once upon a time," he concluded. "At my age, I'm just trying to get out of bed every morning and do what I can to make ends meet. I'm trying to get by with some dignity and, as hokey as this may sound, I want to be able to look upon my baseball life as a good thing. The other 900 ballplayers feel the same way."

Hutto is still waiting for the courtesy of a response.

CHAPTER 2

If you were a casting director doubling as a jury consultant, Fazio and Moran would be the ideal pair of actors you'd choose to co-star as the lead plaintiffs in a class-action lawsuit. Low key and even-keeled to a fault, both like to speak in measured tones. When asked questions, they respond only after first reflecting about how an answer sounds before it comes out of their mouths.

Colbern is nothing like Fazio and Moran.

The proverbial loose cannon, if you attempted to liken Colbern to any one movie character, you'd probably be best served thinking of Bruce Willis' Lieutenant John McClane, from the *Die Hard* film series, to get a handle on his personality.

As Willis tells the villain portrayed by Alan Rickman in the original flick, he is "just a fly in the ointment, Hans. The monkey in the wrench. The pain in the ass."[38]

As far as Colbern goes, that line might not be giving the devil his due.

---

[38] *Die Hard* (1988), Twentieth Century Fox Film Corp.

A native of Santa Monica, California, who was blessed with chiseled good looks in his youth, Colbern played his college ball at Arizona State University (ASU), where he excelled on the baseball diamond and graduated with a degree in criminal justice, which he studied because his father was in law enforcement. That background in criminal justice, he says, is the reason he has always sought justice for people.

Regrettably, once he got to The Show, Colbern never quite realized the potential that he displayed in college. Over the span of two seasons with the White Sox, he played in only 80 games, going 58 for 224 (for a lifetime batting average of .259) with 28 runs batted in (RBIs). Of those hits, 10 were doubles, two were triples and two were homeruns.[39]

Colbern says there's a good reason he never enjoyed greater success—he was always inured because of the position he played, namely, catcher.

Colbern estimates he's had at least a baker's dozen or more surgeries and scopes over the course of his life. According to him, the weight of the mask he wore caused him so much pain that doctors had to remove collagen from his vertebrae in 2001 to ease the pressure on his spine. He's had double rotator cuff surgery. He was operated on to remove bone chips in his left elbow. He had three bulging discs that had to be fused to give his neck greater mobility.

Besides having worn the "tools of ignorance"—that's the term Roger Bresnahan, the Hall of Fame catcher, dubbed catchers' equipment—and the day-to-day rigors that came with playing the demanding position, Colbern says it was all the cortisone and

---

[39] Baseball-Almanac.com

Butazolidin that was injected into him during his playing days that really messed him up.

"I've been on stomach meds for nearly three decades," he said in August 2009, referring to all the Butazolidin he supposedly received from team trainers and doctors. "I've got a hiatal hernia. And I just had an endoscopy to test that I don't have Barrett's esophagus, which is a cancer of the esophagus."

Of all of Colbern's claims, the one that is perhaps the most disconcerting is that there's a proven link between Butazolidin and cancer, and that MLB did not do enough to safeguard the players' interests when team trainers were administering these shots to them.

"The owners were like pushers," he says. "They used us and abused us."

Asked whether there was any truth to Colbern's accusations, that Butazolidin is a carcinogen that could cause Barrett's esophagus, Amy Tieder, a spokesperson for the Mayo Clinic, in Rochester, Minnesota, declined to comment. Dr. Yvonne Romero, of the clinic's Gastroenterology and Hepatology Department, is a leading specialist in the treatment of Barrett's esophagus.

In its annual list of the top hospitals in the country, *U.S. News & World Report* rated the Mayo Clinic as the second best program in the nation for treating digestive disorders. The most recent edition of the list was published in July 2009.

At least one contemporary of Colbern's, Bill Denehy, agrees that MLB did not police cortisone use. How would he know? Over a two-year span in the sixties, Denehy claims he received 57 cortisone injections.

"The trainers used to practice injecting that junk into oranges when we were in the clubhouse," continues Denehy, a recovering alcoholic who claims he's been sober since 1992. "When I was on the stuff, and hit someone, and they rushed the mound, I *wanted* them to rush the mound. I *wanted* them to *fight* me."

As cerebral and, at times, as colorful a figure as any athlete playing today, Denehy and a co-author, Bob Gold, once wrote a book, *Intrinsic Golf—It's Within You: How to Play Better Golf When You Don't Have Time to Practice or Take Lessons* (Trafford Publishing), that he says was inspired by the hitting stroke of the late Hall of Famer, Ted Williams. "The Splendid Splinter," as Williams used to be called, had the sort of rhythmic swing that can be utilized by duffers on the golf course, explains Denehy.

The former Met, Washington Senator and Detroit Tiger hurler is perhaps best known, however, as the player the Mets traded, along with $100,000 in cash, to the Senators for Manager Gil Hodges after the 1967 season.

Denehy, who described himself as the baseball equivalent of a hockey enforcer when he was playing, was no choir boy, that's for sure. In a June 18, 1971 contest between the Tigers and the Cleveland Indians, for example, Indians catcher Ray Fosse charged the mound after getting hit by a pitch thrown by Denehy.

"I'm convinced he was throwing at me and any time a pitcher throws at a batter, he can expect something to happen," Fosse said of Denehy. According to a published account, both benches cleared and swarmed to the mound. Umpire Jim Honochick described the scene as "the bloodiest fight I've seen on a baseball field in 23 years." Denehy then reportedly kicked Fosse in his right hand, causing a gash that required five stitches and sidelining him for more than a week.[40]

Denehy's temper got the best of him when he was out of the majors, too. Once, while serving as the head baseball coach at the University of Hartford, where he coached future Houston Astros star Jeff Bagwell, Denehy made headlines for making comments critical of University of Connecticut assistant baseball coach Mitch Pietras.

"I hope when Pietras comes up to Hartford somebody bombs his car," Denehy said.[41] He was later fired from his job as the Hartford baseball coach when he reportedly added that the entire Connecticut team had "no class."[42]

Besides battling the bottle, Denehy says he's also suffered from periods of depression. But it's his allegations that cortisone is far more hurtful than helpful that are the most troubling.

"I'm not making this up, cortisone does weird stuff to you," says Denehy, who, once he cleaned up his own act, anchored his own graveyard shift talk show and did baseball play-by-play for *Enterprise Radio Network*, in Avon, Connecticut, in the early 1980s. "When Sandy Koufax held his press conference, he talked about the dangers of cortisone use."

He did and he didn't. On November 18, 1966, at the Beverly Wilshire Hotel, Koufax did indeed announce his retirement from the game. But he never specifically pinned the blame on MLB for shortening his career.

---

[40] *New York Times*, "Fosse Sidelined, Bitter at Denehy," June 20, 1971.
[41] *The Washington Post*, April 17, 1987.
[42] Ibid.

The question is, 'Why?' I don't know if cortisone is good for you or not. But to take a shot every other ballgame is more than I wanted to do and to walk around with a constant upset stomach because of the pills and to be high half the time during a ballgame because you're taking painkillers, I don't want to have to do that.[43]

According to a published account, the Academy of Family Physicians recommends that no more than three cortisone shots be administered to the same patient in any one year and no more than ten in a patient's life.[44]

Operated on five years ago to repair a detached retina in one of his eyes, Denehy adds that he developed cataracts in both of them as a result of all the cortisone he was injected with.

Asked to comment about the veracity of Denehy's own allegations, an assistant to Dr. Walter J. Stark, director of the Wilmer Ophthalmological Institute, said Dr. Stark did not have the time to issue a statement. A professor of ophthalmology at the John Hopkins Medical Center, in Baltimore, Maryland, Dr. Stark specializes in cataracts and ophthalmology.

Told that Colbern and Denehy continued to insist that baseball should compensate them, due to the fact they believed all the cortisone injections they received contributed to their current medical problems, Manfred told the author, "Mr. Colbern and Mr. Denehy sued MLB on these claims and lost. As far as we are concerned, the matter is closed."[45]

---

[43] Jane Leavy, "*Sandy Koufax; A Lefty's Legacy,*" Harper Collins Publishers, 2002, p. 237.

[44] Dave Anderson, "Remembering Players M.L.B. Has Forgotten," *New York Times*, March 13, 2004.

[45] November 19, 2009 email to the author.

For the purposes of full disclosure, Colbern, who says he "only" takes 17 different medications each day, none of which are painkillers, freely acknowledges he does see a psychologist on a weekly basis; that he occasionally suffers from pronounced memory loss, that he is treated for sleep apnea and that one of the drugs he takes is to control his bipolar disorder.

Whether or not he is fascinated by the sound of his own voice, or talks more for the shock value than anything else, what is not in dispute is that Colbern has had an especially hard life. After trying to make the California Angels in the spring of 1983, Colbern was released when he wouldn't accept a coaching position. His first wife—the mother of his two daughters, one of whom has cerebral palsy—then filed for divorce six weeks later.

Afterwards, Colbern says he married an ex-girlfriend in Las Vegas specifically to avoid losing his Consolidated Omnibus Budget Reconciliation Act (COBRA) health benefits. Their 2001 marriage lasted 37 days.

Colbern, who says he has sold off most of his baseball memorabilia in order to pay his bills, says he has also been homeless on at least two occasions, the most recent of which was in 2008, when he says he lived on the streets for three weeks. "I used to live in a 4,000 square-foot house," he says. "Now I'm in a 495 square foot apartment and most of my belongings are in a 5' x 5' storage locker."

Colbern says that he has previously received financial aid to pay his rent and phone bills from the Baseball Assistance Team (BAT), the 501(c)(3) charitable organization that has awarded more than $18 million in grants to former members of baseball who are in need. Unfortunately, there is no way to confirm this, since all aid from BAT is strictly confidential.

Though much of his story might engender sympathy, there's a mean-spiritedness to Colbern that has earned him just as many detractors as fans. Driven by an almost single-minded purpose to ensure that the players won in the court of public opinion, if not the court of law, Colbern attempted to enlist the help of those he felt would take the plaintiffs' side in the class-action suit.

The former Sun Devil has bedeviled the media, MLB and the players union ever since.

One of those he lobbied was Maury Brown, the well-respected sports business analyst who founded the Business of Sports Network. Nearly six years later, Brown still recalls feeling uneasy and uncomfortable about what he was being asked to do.

"Mike was very passionate and persistent about this issue," he said in August 2009. "He may fight this battle for the rest of his life."[46]

"I never got the sense that Mike cared about anyone other than himself," continued Brown, who explained that, given the nature of his work, he felt advocating on behalf of the players would compromise his professionalism and objectivity. "It was obvious he felt he deserved compensation for all his injuries."

In terms of sheer snark, however, Colbern's postings on the webblog of the late Doug Pappas are legendary. They are considered so personal that, if you were prepared to give Colbern the benefit of the doubt about all his allegations, his ill will towards Pappas would probably make you start questioning your own sense of decency and moral compass.

A regular contributor to *Baseball Prospectus* who chaired the Business of Baseball Committee of the Society for American

---

[46] Phone conversation with the author on August 7, 2009.

Baseball Research (SABR), and whose analytical work about baseball economics were widely acclaimed—so much so that the Doug Pappas Research Award is presented at SABR's Convention each year—Pappas was a lawyer by profession who on more than one occasion referred to the class-action lawsuit as "frivolous."[47] And Colbern just couldn't resist taking him to task for it:

> Bored to death tonight, which automatically made me think of your writing. I guess I won't need a Sominex tonight. I think I might have made a comment on one of your articles on former players pensions, boy, things are really getting bad if I'm wasting my time that way. Good night Dougie, make sure your Mom tucks you in.[48]

Afterwards, Colbern would actually accuse Pappas of being in league with MLB—a ridiculous assertion considering that Pappas routinely called Selig on the carpet in both his printed and online articles:

> You can see from his article on the pension plight that he did not do his homework and only wrote these two ill-informed articles to curry favor with MLB. Assuming he is a wannabe friend of the MLB attorneys (the real MLB attorneys, not ones who hide behind a hard drive), this hanger-on, this outsider is trying so hard to be recognized and get in the good graces of MLB that he will stoop to calling peers an 'embarrassment to the legal profession' even though this lawsuit not only has merit, but the presiding Judge said the alums were morally in

---

[47] Doug Pappas, "Fan Mail," *Doug's Business of Baseball WebBlog*, May 11, 2004.
[48] Ibid.

the right. He not only writes, but tells anybody who cares to listen that the pension lawsuit is a joke, the attorneys for the alumni are a joke, and that the alumni are tantamount to beggars looking for an undeserved handout. All this to be chummy with real MLB attorneys, guys with class like Rob Manfred.[49]

Colbern saved his most pointed attacks for Acho, whose annual compilations of the top 100 names in college football—he called the list his "All Name Teams"—frequently earned him mentions in *The Detroit News* and on *ESPN* before he discontinued it in 2007.

"Jimmy thought if he just made a big stink about our situation we'd get some publicity, baseball would cave and we'd all get our pensions," says Colbern more than three years after the appeal was denied by the court of appeals for the ninth circuit. "But the discrimination strategy was just stupid.

"I'll give credit where credit is due," he continues. "I didn't know until sometime in August 2003 that the guys in the Negro Leagues had even been awarded any pensions six years earlier by MLB. Jimmy was the one who told us that. But it was the stupidest publicity gimmick you could ever come up with. I mean, who's going to side with a bunch of white guys on this issue?"

Fazio and Moran were referred to Acho by Robert "Bo" Belinsky, the late California Angels hurler who threw a no-hitter against the Baltimore Orioles on May 5, 1962. An employment and labor law specialist with Cummings, McClorey, Davis & Acho (CMDA), a commercial, corporate, business, real estate

---

[49] Doug Pappas, "Now I'm A Shill For MLB!" *Doug's Business of Baseball WebBlog*, May 11, 2004.

and defense litigation law firm based in Livonia, Michigan that was co-founded in 1965 by his father, Ronald, Acho worked as a prosecuting attorney for Redford Township, in Wayne County, Michigan, prior to joining CMDA.

With an impressive number of high-profile cases to his credit, including the dropping of criminal charges against Detroit Lions linebacker Larry Foote, who was arrested following a brawl at a restaurant in 2003, when he was a member of the Pittsburgh Steelers, Acho seemed a natural choice to handle the class-action suit, especially given all the work he had done with Barney to attempt to increase the pensions of NFL retirees.

Strictly speaking, no matter how much he may have sympathized with Fazio and Moran, Acho had no business taking up their cause; according to him, CMDA had enjoyed a long-standing professional relationship with the Detroit Tigers club, which was named as one of the defendants in the class-action suit. That's why, to avoid even the appearance of a conflict of interest, Rumsey was brought in to be the attorney of record for the plaintiffs.

Advised that Colbern feels his strategy was a loser from the start, Acho counters that he and Rumsey "did what we felt we had to do. The statute of limitations had long run against MLBPA so there was no suit there. But there was a cause of action against MLB still viable, and we took a shot.[50]

"The MLBPAA told these men for years they were close to getting a pension worked out, and it never happened," continues Acho. "The retirees begged me to file that suit. Trust me, filing was not the first thing on my mind, especially against such a formidable foe, but we saw it was inevitable.

[50] August 11, 2009 email to the author.

"The case did have merit," Acho explains, "but the goal was that MLB would be tried and found liable in the court of public opinion, and that sentiment would side with our guys and MLB would give in and offer up something to these men. It didn't happen."

MLB seems to have recognized right from the start that the plaintiffs had a weak case against the owners. In one of the earliest letters from the Office of the Commissioner about this matter, on February 14, 2003, Manfred tells Acho, "I view your threats of a 'public relations campaign' and 'possible legal action' to be singularly inappropriate."

Six months later, in a letter dated August 12, 2003, Manfred continued to come across as the voice of reason by counseling Acho that it would be wrong to file the lawsuit. "I find your threat to commence a lawsuit against Major League Baseball to be somewhat puzzling given the fact that you repeatedly recognized, during our earlier conversation, that you had no viable legal claim against Major League Baseball," he wrote. "While you did assert that even in the absence of a viable legal claim, you were prepared to file a lawsuit for publicity purposes, I would urge you to consider carefully the wisdom of that course of action."

"I do my due diligence," maintained Acho in defense of the work he did on behalf of the ballplayers. "I don't just file lawsuits cavalierly. We spoke to some of the top sports law and entertainment lawyers in the country and looked at lawsuits filed before us before we did anything. We did research, spoke to the American Medical Association and doctors about cortisone shots. Please. No firms out there would have done a more competent job for these men then ours and DaCorsi, Placencio and Rumsey did and I'm sure Mike knows this."

Acho isn't losing any sleep over Colbern's disparaging remarks, however. "I'm pretty thick skinned," says Acho. "I know how Mike is, and deep down he appreciates us, I know it."

Moran, for one, thinks Colbern is "off the wall," and that his complaints about Acho are baseless. "Jimmy did a great job of getting this thing going," says Moran of Acho's efforts. However, he concedes that an alternative approach, one that was less antagonistic, might have been warranted.

"We had no business doing this," says Moran, of the lawsuit. "It got spurs under the league's saddle. But we were ticked off, and we're still ticked off."

Even the normally circumspect Fazio wonders whether the players should have done things differently. "Baseball didn't like that we got lawyers involved and that we went to court," he said three years after the fact. "It obviously didn't help us any, the way things turned out."

In *Overlawyered*, which bills itself as the oldest legal blog on the World Wide Web, attorney Ted Frank practically channeled Pappas in denouncing the players' attempts to get a pension. "In their world, it's unlawful discrimination to negotiate better benefits for current employees without making those benefits retroactive for all existing retirees," he wrote. "In our world, it's not."[51]

When asked his opinion about the case, a well-regarded, nationally syndicated weekly sports business columnist who is an assistant professor at a mid-western university, where he teaches

---

[51] Ted Frank, "Three Former Players Sue MLB Over Pension," *Overlawyered*, November 8, 2003.

courses on ethics and sports marketing, expressed incredulousness that the players association wasn't named as a co-defendant.

"The union sold these players down the river during the 1980 strike negotiations," said the author, a lawyer by profession who formerly owned and operated two minor league baseball teams. They should harbor at least some of the responsibility for the players' predicament, he continued.

Why wasn't the MLBPA named as a co-defendant? As Acho notes, the statute of limitations had run out against the union. But there might have been another reason to explain the glaring omission.

In a letter dated September 26, 2003, Michael S. Weiner, the current executive director of the MLBPA who was then the union's associate general counsel, tells Acho "we have never been advised of any legal theory on which you could base a colorable claim against the MLBPA." Just like MLB's Manfred, Weiner adds, "we are not aware of any plausible legal argument that such a claim would be viable.

"We are writing to inform you that the suit you intend to file against the MLBPA... would be brought in bad faith and in order to harass," he continues. "Please be advised that if you do indeed file such a suit we will seek sanctions and other available penalties under Rule 11 of the Federal Rules of Civil Procedure, under Michigan Rule of Professional Conduct 3.1, and through any other avenues which may be available to us."

The threat of being sanctioned did not dissuade Acho, whose reply to Weiner a week later was typically forceful.

"At this time we are not pursuing the MLBPA, but please do not think that your inappropriate, unprofessional and misguided threats to us are what lead to that decision," he countered in his October 2, 2003 letter. "I would strongly advise you to not worry about me or this law firm, or threaten us, and instead focus on the task at hand—that is, the Union's responsibility to these 1,053 men."

Is it possible that Acho didn't name the union as a codefendant in the suit because he feared that he might be censored or, still worse, disbarred? And what about Weiner's intimation that the union might file a civil suit against CMDA?

Obviously, though anything is possible, it's more likely that Acho didn't try to involve the players association because of his stated explanation, namely, that the statute of limitations had simply run out.

As for the lawsuit itself, the same sports columnist, who spoke on the condition of anonymity, added that, "it was a dog to begin with.

"In effect, these players argued that they were the victims of reverse discrimination, and that argument just wasn't going to hold water," says the professor. "In today's post-racial climate, it certainly wouldn't have any merit."

In fact, upon learning of Justice Real's decision, the lawyer for MLB, Howard Ganz, of Proskauer Rose Goetz & Mendelsohn, a firm well known for representing professional sports organizations, went out of his way to chastise the players for likening their situation to that of the former Negro Leaguers.

"Baseball, in an effort to at least repair some of the actions or inactions of many decades before, decided to do something that would be beneficial for those who played in the Negro Leagues and had been excluded from major league baseball," he said. "And for the plaintiffs here to try to capitalize upon that seems to me totally inappropriate."[52]

No less than Pappas himself called the legal strategy "offensive. MLB had voluntarily credited former Negro Leaguers, who had been systematically excluded from MLB because of their race, with their Negro League service time for purposes of determining pension and benefit eligibility, therefore, MLB was now discriminating against Caucasians by not paying plaintiffs benefits they hadn't earned."[53]

Pappas seemed particularly irked by the website that Acho and Rumsey paid a University of Michigan student, Doug Gnodtke, to build in order to promote their case.

> As confirmed by the website created by plaintiffs to promote their demands, plaintiffs' real goal was to fill the media with sob stories about impoverished ex-players, creating so much negative publicity that MLB and/or the MLBPA would pay them to go away. Instead they've been thrown out of court. Yes, it's a shame that some former major leaguers live in poverty. But it's a shame that anyone in this country lives in poverty.[54]

"It's not discriminatory to treat Player A, a mediocrity who couldn't hold a roster spot long enough to qualify for his pension differently from Player B, who would have qualified for his pension if not for the institutional racism which barred him from the roster," reasoned Pappas.[55]

[52] Michael R. Blood, "Former Baseball Players Lose Bid For Pensions, Benefits," *The Associated Press*, March 16, 2004.
[53] Doug Pappas, "Former Players Lose Bid For Pensions, Benefits," *Doug's Business of Baseball WebBlog*, March 16, 2004.
[54] Ibid.
[55] Ibid.

In hindsight, Pappas may have been a bit harsh in his assessment, since many of these ballplayers did have fine, albeit brief, careers that they're very proud of. Yes, the color of their skin did not automatically bar them from playing in The Show. And yes, their years of service fell short of the vesting requirement needed to be awarded a pension. But a blanket indictment characterizing them all as mediocrities is just as mean-spirited as, say, what one might expect to hear coming out of the mouth of Colbern.

Ironically, the website is where both Pappas and Colbern, the two long-time antagonists, found common ground. Colbern also thought the now-defunct site, *www.baseballpension.com*, shouldn't have aired the players' grievances.

"How does hiring some computer geek help get us our benefits?" he asks.

Acho can only sing the praises of Gnodtke, who is now the Associate Director of Athletics at the State University of New York at Buffalo.

"(Doug) is a rising star in collegiate athletics who set up the site, and it was an excellent site and source of info," gushes Acho. "It was a great site that we could afford to set up."

Even Weiner expressed outrage about the site. "We request that you immediately cease using (former MLBPA executive director) Don Fehr's name and picture in the 'lineup' on your website," he wrote Acho. "Such use is misleading in that it suggests that Mr. Fehr endorses your positions."

Acho does regret one thing—that he wasn't able to help get these ballplayers the monies he sincerely feels they deserve.

"MLB and MLBPA turned their back on these men and have done so for three decades," he says. "These men should be receiving a pension of $10,000 annually and medical benefits. Period. I hope the MLBPAA can get it done. And if they do, it was our work that was the impetus."

CHAPTER 3

Growing up in Billings, Montana six decades ago, Neibauer lived only three blocks from Cobb Field, the historic stadium built in 1932 that was destroyed in 2007. Once home to the Billings Mustangs, the Cincinnati Reds' Pioneer League Rookie Affiliate, Neibauer fondly recalls sitting in the famous wood stands during rain delays and gaining an appreciation for the game of baseball.

"There's nothing like it," he says. "Its grace, its beauty. The sport continues to thrill me no end."

Like Qualls, who debuted with the Cubs in 1969, Neibauer enjoyed modest success as a rookie, going 1-2 that year while posting a respectable 3.90 ERA for the Braves in 29 games. He capped off his first season by throwing a hitless, scoreless inning against the Mets in the National League Championship Series.

All told, Neibauer went 4-8 during his playing days with a 4.78 ERA. He would later work as a scout for the Texas Rangers before beginning his second career as a mortgage broker.

In the summer of 2009, his salad days long behind him, Neibauer—one of the rare 10 percent of the population who isn't obese but nonetheless suffers from type 2 diabetes—was living and working in Aurora, Colorado. Married to Christine Law, an elder care attorney, Neibauer, who also has two metal prostheses in his hips, was supplementing his income by running instructional pitching clinics for the Marc Johnson Sports Center. He estimates that each week he gives lessons to some 25 to 30 pupils, both young and old alike, who receive the benefit of his wisdom. "My oldest student," he says with a laugh, "is a pilot for United Airlines."

More than 35 years after his last game, Neibauer, who lettered in four sports at the University of Nebraska, is asked if he can still bring the heat. "I can still get somebody's attention if I wanted to," he says with pride.

He's now trying to do just that, for all the former players like himself who are without pensions.

As one of four members of the special MLBPAA committee attempting to ensure that the men named in the class-action suit finally receive their pensions, Neibauer is especially bothered by what he says is the perception that the alumni group was in some way responsible for the lawsuit. "To this day, I believe MLB and the union feel that the alumni were behind it," he says. "Nothing could be further from the truth."

While Neibauer mostly characterizes the baseball community as "great," he remains mystified why certain parties have not taken up the cause of the pre-1980, non-vested players. Baseball beat writers, for example.

With the exception of journalists such as Dave Anderson, of the *New York Times*, or John McGrath, of the *Tacoma News*

Tribune, few columnists and broadcasters who cover the 30 teams have written or reported about this matter over the years. Only half-kiddingly, Neibauer says that, when he and the other committee members "tried to enlist the sports writers to help us in this effort, we found out that all the free beer and finger sandwiches, provided by the teams after games, was too much for us to overcome."

Even Hall of Famers who subsequently exchanged their pitching mounds for soap boxes were reluctant to take a stance. When he wrote then United States Representative Jim Bunning about this issue more than a decade ago, Neibauer received a response, dated April 14, 1998, that was short and to the point.

"Unfortunately," the future United States Senator from Kentucky indicated, "I don't feel I can be of any help."

Neibauer was taken aback. This was, after all, the same public servant who had always been at the forefront of retiree issues, who had served as the chairman of the House Ways and Means Subcommittee on Social Security until 1999. And Bunning didn't feel *he* could be of assistance?

At least Neibauer *received* a personal reply. When Acho was attempting to get a written statement or affidavit from the senator in support of his clients more than five years later, he butted heads with Richard L. Robinson, of the law firm of Graydon, Head, Ritchey, LLP, over his plans to depose Bunning once the trial started.

"I do plan on deposing the Senator… and you've said you'd file a motion to quash," wrote Acho on September 17, 2003. "Well, that's your right, but I don't think you have a leg to stand on."

Fast forward six years into the future, and time still hadn't changed Bunning much. Repeated efforts by the author in the summer of 2009 to contact the senator at his then district office proved fruitless, as well.

Neibauer is perhaps most confused by the union's continued aversion to giving the ex-ballplayers pensions. "The union has been so aggressive in not wanting us to get pensions," he said. "Their position makes no sense to me whatsoever.

"The approach of the Alumni Association has always been a rational one, to quietly go about building support for our effort, which of course was in direct contrast to the lawsuit," he continued. "That's what irritated me so much about the lawsuit. We've never made any waves."

"The association has been working behind the scenes on this issue for the last 14 years," agreed Eddie Robinson, another one of the MLBPAA pension committee members who, after his own playing days ended, in 1957, continued in the game in an assortment of jobs. "We'd wait three or four years for MLB to come through for the guys, and they'd say, 'It isn't the right time.' Well, when is it ever gonna be the right time? You can't wait too long, especially with so many of the fellers dying."

A four-time All-Star who, in 1951, batted .282, drove in 117 runs and smashed 29 home runs, Robinson's post-playing career included serving as a coach with the Baltimore Orioles, a player development consultant with the Houston Astros, a farm system director for the Kansas City Athletics and, finally, as the general manager of both the Atlanta Braves, from 1972 through 1976, and Texas Rangers, from 1978-1982.

If there is indeed a golden thread that intertwines all of us together, as the late John Ritter once observed, then it is not terribly surprising that Robinson knows so many of the principals

DOUGLAS J. GLADSTONE | 69

involved in this matter. For instance, Robinson played a significant role in Fazio's development after the Colt .45s signed him.

Similarly, when Neibauer blew out the tendons in his pitching arm as a member of the 1972 Phillies—the team which had the most losses ever for a single season with a pitcher, Hall of Famer Steve Carlton, who led the league in victories that year—he was relieved to learn that the Braves later purchased his contract back from Philadelphia.

The person who told him that he was returning to Atlanta was none other than Robinson. "I was convinced my career was all but over," says Neibauer. "It's funny how life works. Eddie helped rescue me from a bad situation and now we're working together to try to rescue other guys."

"I really respect the owners, and I'm convinced that MLB has a willingness to do the right thing by these players, I really do," says Robinson, who in the summer of 2009 was 88-years-old and could have just as easily decided not to care about anyone but his immediate family. A native of Texas who grows pecans on his 200-acre farm in Bastrop, near Austin, he and his wife, Bette, raised four sons, one of whom played professional baseball in the Phillies system and another who was a running back and field goal kicker for the Pittsburgh Steelers.

As someone who *is* receiving a pension, Robinson has an appreciation for history. "In 1989, our pensions weren't really worth a lot," he remembers. "Then Early Wynn got interested in our situation. Imagine that? A Hall of Famer took the time to care about us little guys.

"Well, after Wynn got involved, Fehr took a proposal to the owners, and we got substantial raises," continues Robinson. "I always appreciated that. And that's sort of why I'm doing this now. I want to help these guys get what's long overdue them, just like Wynn helped me."

To say the 1990 increase was substantial would be an understatement. According to a published account, the collective bargaining agreement hammered out at that time allowed widows to draw their husbands' full pensions, instead of about half the amount as before, while pensions for players with 10 years of service who retired at age 50 before 1959 jumped from $650 to $1,394 a month, or $16,728 a year.[56]

Given the economy's downward spiral, is it feasible to believe the players' union could hammer out such a deal today? The third member of the Alumni Association committee working diligently to get pensions for the non-vested, pre-1980 players definitely thinks so.

As far as money still being plentiful and in abundance, little has changed in the last two decades, according to David Clyde, the onetime phenom for the Texas Rangers who was only 37 days shy of being fully vested when he retired from the game in 1981, while he was in the Houston Astros minor league farm system.

"Don't tell me there's no money to do this thing," argued Clyde, who compiled an 18-33 record in 84 starts with the Rangers and Cleveland during his time in The Show. "They're signing kids to outrageous contracts and selling teams for ungodly purchase prices," he said for added emphasis.

Clyde was referring to the record four-year, $15.1 million deal that Stephen Strasburg, of the San Diego State Aztecs,

[56] "Sports People: Baseball; More Pension Benefits Awarded To Old Timers," *The New York Times*, August 23, 1990.

received in August 2009 from the Washington Nationals, which eclipsed the $10.5 million given to Mark Prior by the Cubs in 2001, as well as the Tribune Company's same month sale of the Cubs to Joe Ricketts, the founder of the online brokerage house, TD Ameritrade Holding Corporation, for $845 million.

Clyde knows a thing or two about signing bonuses, since he was the number-1 overall choice in the 1973 draft, and an instant idol when he joined the Rangers for a reported $125,000 bonus.[57] Former Kansas City Royals, St. Louis Cardinals and Texas Rangers manager Whitey Herzog, who will be inducted into the Hall of Fame on the last weekend in July this year, even called the hard-throwing product of Westchester High School one of the best young lefthanders he had ever seen.[58]

These days, Clyde is idolized by a whole new group of fans. On a warm summer afternoon in August 2009, Clyde can be found barking out instructions to a group of youngsters he regularly gives pitching lessons to in Houston, Texas. "Turn your hips and shoulders," he screams at one charge. "Stay straight over your back legs," he lectures another. "Relax, don't lean back," he says to a third. Still the same straight shooter he was during his playing days, Clyde is not shy about the reason he wants to see justice done.

"There are a lot of guys who were not nearly as fortunate nor nearly as blessed as I've been," says Clyde, who is the pitching coach for The Houston Miracles, a Christian—based team of high schoolers. "Giving 'em all pensions is the least MLB can do when some of the guys are begging for Hamburger Helper.

---

[57] Kyle Ringo, "Turn Back The Clock," *Baseball Digest*, August 2003.
[58] Dave Anderson, "Sports of The Times; The Mismanaged Career of David Clyde," *New York Times*, June 22, 2003.

"I've told both Fehr and Rogers (former Montreal Expos pitcher Steve Rogers handles pensions issues for the players association) to their faces on at least two separate occasions that I don't need the pension. Understand? Some of these 900 guys actually *need* it. Hell, I'd *like* one, but I don't *need* one. That's the difference."

At the MLBPAA board meeting held in Houston in January 2009, Clyde apparently did more than just express his opinion about the matter to Rogers. According to one person who witnessed their conversation, Clyde "lit up Rogers' ass like a Christmas tree."

To be fair, this same eyewitness, who spoke on the condition of anonymity, considers Rogers "an asshole." Nonetheless, Clyde does not deny the exchange took place.

"You know, I can be a nice guy," says Clyde, recalling the incident. "The alumni have tried to go about doing things the right way, we haven't tried to ruffle any feathers, but the long and the short of it is that nothing has gotten done with the owners.

"We've been relying on the owners' sense of fairness for nearly 30 years," he continued. "And I just feel that either we're not being told the truth, or people are paying us lip service. So just tell me the truth and don't lie to me anymore, that's all I ask for. Just tell me the truth."

Truth of the matter is, besides wanting to right a wrong that's been perpetrated against himself and his baseball brothers, Clyde is also motivated to help these men get pensions because he feels a bit guilty; when he was first called up to the big leagues, in June 1973, the phenom apparently took the roster spot of a Texas Ranger who never satisfied the four-year vesting requirement himself, and who later died from cancer.

While Clyde doesn't know whom he replaced, an educated guess would be Joe Lovitto, the speedy outfielder who played in only 26 games for Texas during the 1973 season and who later died from cancer at the age of 50. Though Lovitto played full seasons for the Rangers in both 1972 and 1974, he was often on the disabled list in 1975, when he was on the Mets roster, and only played in 50 games. Since he was released the following spring training, in all likelihood he did not have the four years needed to qualify for a pension.

A man's man who believes that one's word is his bond, Clyde feels that not enough owners "man up," as it were.

"At some function I was attending I was standing so close to both (Houston Astros owner) Dayton McLane and (Texas Rangers owner) Tom Hicks that you could smell what was on their breath," said Clyde. "And Hicks looks me straight in the eye and says to me, 'There's no reason you shouldn't have a job in baseball so you can get that remaining service credit.' Looked me straight in the eye when he said it. And neither of 'em are returning my calls now."

Once his playing days ended, Clyde tried desperately to get a position—any position—in baseball in order to stay in the game. "Hell, if need be, I was willing to sweep toilets in rookie league to get back in the game," said Clyde, only half-jokingly.

Luckily, his ex-wife's family ran a lumber business, and he worked at that job for almost two decades, retiring in 2003. But old slights linger; even now, Clyde is not able to mask his disappointment that MLB hasn't been able to offer him or any of his comrades a helping hand.

"I think the owners are prepared to drag their feet on this issue for a long time," he says. "After all, the longer it takes for this to be resolved, the less people they have to pay. Maybe that's been their strategy all along."

As for Clyde's feelings regarding the union, he credits Fehr for exerting an almost Svengali-like influence over the players during his run as executive director of the players association.

"I don't believe today's players have a clue as to what's going on and what's happening to the guys who played before them," he said. "I don't think they know *anything* about our situation. In fact, I think if Don Fehr had told all the players to walk off a cliff that was 700 feet high up in the air, and told them that, if they did, they'd all get a share of $10 million, I think they'd all walk off that cliff together," he added.

While that may speak volumes about player solidarity today, it means absolutely nothing to the ballplayers of yesteryear, who aren't earning the major league minimum of $390,000.[59] As of 2007, the average salary of a major leaguer baseball player was $2.8 million.[60]

Chances are pretty good that the fourth member of the alumni association committee, Skok, never made *half* that much money during his *entire* four-season career. A former middle-reliever who pitched for the Boston Red Sox, Texas Rangers and Atlanta Braves, Skok's record during his playing days was 4-7 with a 4.86 ERA; all told, he had five saves in 107 appearances, striking out 85 batters in a total of 150 innings of work.

---

[59] Frequently Asked Questions, MLB.com/pa.
[60] Ibid.

Like Robinson, Skok is attempting to see that these men get a pension even though he himself already receives one. The chairman of the alumni association's services committee, Skok has for more than two decades been working to find ways to better the lives of former players. For instance, baseball alumni now have access to heart, lung and vascular care at the Deborah Heart & Lung Center, in Brown Mills, New Jersey, thanks to the partnership between the facility and the alumni association.

"This is just a natural progression of the work I've been doing all along," says Skok, who resides in Atlanta, Georgia and is a sales representative for a global manufacturer of connector products when he's not helping former players. Taking up their cause, he adds, is just the right thing to do.

"I suppose I could have chosen to sit on the sidelines," he says, "but that's not my style."

Known as a crafty lefthander when he pitched, Skok showed the same type of craftiness and moxy when his own career was winding down. According to the *Los Angeles Times*, Skok in 1980 placed a call to Ted Turner, then the Atlanta Braves' owner, when he was in the minors and two weeks shy of the four years he needed to be eligible for a pension. Turner agreed to put the left-hander in the Braves' bullpen and, even though Skok never entered a game, that's how he qualified for his $1,000 monthly payment.[61]

Nearly 30 years later, Skok concedes that, if he hadn't called Turner, he "probably wouldn't be getting a pension. That's why it's important to fight for all those guys who aren't getting theirs."

---

[61] Greg Johnson, "Systems of Checks and Imbalances," *Los Angeles Times*, February 27, 2007.

"We've tried to do this diplomatically for a long time," says Skok of the alumni association's interactions with both MLB and the players' union on the matter of the pre-1980, non-vested players. "For the most part, we've come hat in hand and very humbly asked that the right thing be done for these guys. But we've been put off and stalled every way possible. We've heard every excuse in the book. Well, enough is enough."

Perhaps fittingly, since he is originally from Dobbs Ferry, New York, the place where, in August 1781, continental army troops commanded by George Washington developed a plan of attack that would ultimately win the Revolutionary War, Skok in the summer of 2009 knew he, Neibauer, Robinson and Clyde would have to ratchet up the pressure if the ballplayers were ever to receive their pensions. Plotting their strategy via regular conference calls, the four committee members debated what the best course of action would be.

What they agreed upon in August of that year was to first send a letter to the 874 pre-1980, non-vested players seeking support for their efforts.

"There is no question that MLB and the union enjoy great success today, in part because of your efforts," the letter indicated. "We believe that the best way for MLB and the union to show their appreciation for your past contributions is to support our continuing efforts to have your group of former Major League Baseball players participate in the Major League Players benefits plan or receiving other appropriate benefits and services in recognition of your efforts."

Sensing they needed a catchphrase that would ignite interest in their cause, the foursome quickly dubbed their initiative *Raise the Bar with Benefits, Assistance and Recognition Before the Final Out.*

In Centralia, Washington, Darcy Fast, the Senior Pastor at the Centralia Community Church of God, was informed about the letter the quartet would soon be sending him and shook his head in disbelief. The former Cub, who voluntarily hung up his spikes at the age of 24, was confident that Skok, Neibauer, Robinson and Clyde were well-intentioned, principled individuals who merely wanted to help their fellow man. What he couldn't fathom was why, after nearly 30 years, neither MLB nor the union had taken any corrective actions to remedy the situation.

"I just can't believe that MLB wouldn't take care of these guys," said Fast, a lefthander who played in eight games for the Cubs in 1968 and whom Manager Leo Durocher was reportedly counting on to pitch during the 1969 season.[62] Unfortunately for the Cubs, who could have used him once Chicago's lead over the Mets began to shrink that year, Fast was drafted into the army.

"I always believed fulfilling my military obligation to this country was of paramount importance," continues Fast, who wrote a book, *The Missing Cub*, that described his adventures away from the sport. "Maybe that's why I never counted on a pension in the first place."

Fast ultimately did return from his tour of duty but by then, he wasn't thinking about baseball. Motivated by a higher calling, Fast went to seminary school and followed in his father's footsteps by becoming a minister.

"I have not lived my life to get a pension from MLB," adds Fast. "The way I see it, I gave up something really good to get

---

[62] Neil Hayes, "Fast Rise, Fast To Exit for Former Cubs Pitcher," Chicago *Sun Times*, May 15, 2008.

something even better. So I've got no complaints. But I do regret that those guys who do have medical problems aren't being helped by MLB.

"It seems that the ballplayers of today just don't care," continues Fast. "It appears that nobody cares about all those guys who played years ago."

It is a sentiment echoed by 74-year-old Tom Qualters, who allowed six earned runs when he made his major league debut on September 13, 1953. The only pitcher to appear on a Topps baseball card four times without recording a win or a loss during his career, Qualters was nicknamed "Money Bags" because he was a bonus baby signed right out of high school by the Phillies for the then-princely sum of $40,000.

"There are a lot of good people in baseball," says Qualters, who would enjoy his best season in 1958, when he appeared in 26 games and hurled 43 innings for the Chicago White Sox. "What's sad and what irritates me the most is that, given all the money the owners are throwing around nowadays, you would think that they could fund pensions for all these guys who aren't getting them."

Qualters does receive a pension, but it's as a result of his career in government, not his time in The Show. After hanging up his spikes and trying his hand at a variety of jobs, including the oil business, Qualters took a civil service test and wound up working as a law enforcement agent for the Pennsylvania Fish and Boat Commission, where it was his responsibility to protect wildlife. "I was always running into the woods when I was a kid," he reminisced, "so this really was my dream job. I was the luckiest guy in the world."

Out of professional baseball more than five decades, when he's not fishing or on the fairways—Qualters says he has an 18 handicap and consistently shoots in the mid-eighties—the active septuagenarian still manages to remain close to the game. He's a volunteer coach for both the Somerset High School and Somerset American Legion baseball squads.

Of the chances he'll ever collect a retirement allowance from MLB, Qualters remains less than enthusiastic. "It's gotten to the point where I feel we're not going to get anything from them," he says.

"I thought maybe everything would work out one day, but I just finally quit trying to get the money," agrees 72-year-old Don Dillard, who hung up his spikes in 1965. "Besides, at my age, I'm just not able to remember all the people who I contacted to try to help me."

A fourth outfielder and pinch-hitter extraordinaire who played with the Cleveland Indians and Milwaukee Braves for parts of six seasons, Dillard's best campaigns were while he was playing for The Tribe in 1961 and 1962, when he came up to bat a combined 318 times and hit 12 homeruns. All told, when Dillard's career came to an end, he had played in 272 games, gotten 116 hits and wound up with a lifetime batting average of .244.

Now a resident of Waterloo, South Carolina, where he and his 70-year-old wife, Elma, run a mobile home trailer park that he says is always filled to capacity, Dillard notes he never made more than $9,500 while playing the game he loves.

"Our house is paid for and our kids are all grown and married, so we're doing alright," says Dillard. "But because I don't get a pension, we're lucky we have that trailer park, it's a huge part of our income."

How close was Dillard to receiving a benefit allowance? According to him, he received an April 22, 1974 letter from the league's retirement plans administrator that indicated he was only 17 days shy of the vesting requirement, which had been lowered to four years' service in 1969.

"I never really started trying to get one (a pension) until after I got that letter," he added. "That and the fact I saw Al Cicotte on the Yankees bench after he was already supposed to have been retired for a decade."

A great-nephew of Eddie Cicotte, one of the infamous players on the Chicago White Sox accused of throwing the 1919 World Series to the Cincinnati Reds, Al Cicotte was a pitcher originally drafted by the Yankees in 1948 who didn't debut in the big leagues until 1957. After bouncing around the majors with five other teams, Cicotte's last game was with the Houston Colt .45s in 1962.

While he was home watching a "Game of the Week" on television one Saturday afternoon in the early 1970s, Dillard says he spotted Cicotte in a Yankees uniform in the dugout. Only eight games shy of a pension, Dillard says that Cicotte must have convinced the Bronx Bombers to create a roster spot for him. "I call it *gratis* time," he adds.

Dillard says that, a few years later, when he asked his former Indians teammate, Chuck Tanner, then the manager of the Atlanta Braves, to do the same thing for him, Tanner initially agreed to help him out. According to Dillard, Tanner told him a Braves coach was having surgery that summer, and that the club would sign him on an interim basis.

"But Bobby Cox (the then-general manager of the Braves) didn't go for it," he continued. According to Dillard, Cox killed the idea because he believed promoting a coach within the ranks of the organization was the right thing to do.

In effect, Dillard tried to do the same thing that both Cicotte and Skok had done. It's also what the Braves did for Satchel Paige when the future Hall of Famer was signed by Atlanta at the tail end of the 1968 season. Needing 158 days on a big league payroll to qualify for a pension, Paige never pitched for the club but, instead, became a coach who stayed on through the following season.

"I won't starve, I'm not a pauper, and I don't live hand to mouth, but I just feel I'm due something," says Dillard. Especially because he claims his career was shortened after a freak play on the base paths caused him to suffer permanent double vision.

In a Braves game against the Los Angeles Dodgers, Dillard says he was on base after getting a single when the next batter hit what he recalls was a fairly easy grounder to Maury Wills, the National League's Most Valuable Player in 1962. Wills also won a Gold Glove Award that same season for his fielding play at shortstop.

What happened next is anybody's guess, because Dillard says several Braves players told him later that he got hit in the head and lay unconscious on the ground for a long time. "When I came to," he says, "my teammates were standing over me between first and second base. That's where they say I was tagged out for the last out of the inning."

Though he doesn't actually recall what happened, Dillard says his teammates told him in the dugout afterwards that, instead of just stepping on the bag or flipping the ball to the second baseman, Wills opted to try to throw the batter out at first. "I'm still amazed that he just didn't step on the bag for the force out," says Dillard.

Dillard, who says he had broken his stride running to second base, admits he wasn't really running all that hard. "There were already two outs and I just naturally assumed Willis was going to force me at second base," he says. "But his throw was so wild that, if the ball hadn't hit me in the head, the guys told me it would have gone into either the dugout or the stands."

"That play really bothered me," admits Dillard. "The first thing I thought was that maybe Wills was retaliating for something I once did to him, but I wasn't a dirty player. So I guess the ball just plain slipped out of his hand when he went to throw it."

Either way, to this day, Dillard says his eyesight is so bad because of the double vision that "it's sort of like seeing two of everything coming right at you all the time." He says his stigmatism really acts up whenever he walks into a movie theatre and has to adjust his eyes to the dark.

After all this time, getting a pension would be wonderful, says Dillard. "At my age, something would be better than nothing," he said. "I'm not expecting one, but I'd be tickled pink to get anything."

Former St. Louis Cardinals pitcher Lloyd Merritt isn't expecting a pension from MLB either, but said he'd like to see "all those guys who just came up short of their four years get it first.

"I'd feel better if I knew they were taken care of," continued Merritt, who said he was "flabbergasted" upon learning that MLB had awarded payments to the Negro Leaguers.

Originally signed by the Yankees, Merritt says he won 22 games in the Piedmont League one year but wasn't able to duplicate his minor league success with any consistency after Uncle Sam drafted him. Though he saved seven games and posted a more than respectable 3.31 ERA in the 44 games he pitched in 1957, the St. Louis native didn't make his hometown club out of spring training the following season.

"I was privileged and honored to play the game for that one year," said the 76-year-old Merritt. "So I feel my service credit is just as good as anyone else's."

The four alumni committee members want Merritt to be rewarded for that credit. "I'm cautiously optimistic," says Skok. "But in my heart of hearts, I just don't know."

Skok had good reason to hedge his bets. In June 2009, the executive director of the alumni association, Dan Foster, did not even acknowledge that Skok, Neibauer, Clyde and Robinson were having conference calls regarding the issue. "The matter of obtaining some form of financial consideration for the inactive, non-vested pre-1980 player is one that the association feels very passionate about," he said in an official statement. "We have been in ongoing discussions with MLB ownership and the Players Association for quite sometime and we continue in this effort."[63]

---

[63] June 25, 2009 email to the author.

Second

CHAPTER 4

"Baseball Pension Strategy: Wait Out The Old Timers," screamed the newspaper headline in bold typeface. The story, carried in the *Los Angeles Times,* told the now familiar tale of ballplayers who felt they had been treated shabbily by both the players association and MLB.[64]

The date the article ran? It was June 15, 1997.

More than a decade ago, a whole different group of ex-major leaguers also believed that both the union and the owners had done them wrong. The difference was, these retired players were those whose careers ended before 1947, when baseball's pension fund was first created.

Baseball's second commissioner, Happy Chandler, like Bunning a former United States senator from Kentucky, had previously served as governor and had worked to see to it that teachers in that state received pensions.[65] As commissioner, the plan he unveiled in 1947 guaranteed that each player who had five years of

[64] Hal Bock, *The Associated Press,* June 15, 1997.
[65] Richard Barbieri, *Hardball Times,* April 24, 2009.

service would receive a check for $50 a month at age 50, and then ten dollars a month over the next five years.[66]

More than two decades later, in 1969, the five-year vesting requirement was reduced to four years of service. And, of course, 11 years after that, the requirement was again amended so that all a player has needed since 1980 is one day of service credit for health benefits and 43 days of service credit to be eligible for a retirement allowance.

The pension fund, which was started with monies Chandler helped negotiate for radio rights to the World Series in 1947, [67] was initially set up for $650,000, with teams providing 80 percent and the players investing the remaining 20 percent.[68] And two years later, in 1949, Chandler arranged a lucrative $4.375 million deal for the radio rights to the Series for next seven years.[69] The next season, the commissioner outdid himself by securing a deal worth one million dollars a year for the next six years of World Series television rights, which also went directly to the players' pension fund.[70]

The problem was, Chandler and the owners had decided that players would be eligible to receive a pension only if they were on a team roster on the last day of the 1946 season or the first day of the 1947 season.[71]

Consequently, Carl Hubbell, who was inducted into the Hall of Fame in 1947, never got a pension because he won his 253 big league games before 1947; however, under the current rules,

[66] Baseball Almanac.
[67] Ibid.
[68] Barbieri, *Hardball Times*, April 24, 2009.
[69] Ibid.
[70] Ibid.
[71] Brian Jenkins, "Old-time Major Leaguer Fights For Pension," CNN, October 21, 1996.

former Twin Terry Felton, who compiled an 0-16 record during the 1980s, does receive one.[72]

Even Selig recognized the inequity. "It's categorically unfair," he told Dave Anderson, the Pulitzer Prize-winning columnist of the *New York Times*. "In the next labor contract, there should be a provision" for the pre-1947 players.[73]

Just like with the pre-1980 players, the union argued at the time that the players association lacked the authority, either under the CBA or under the law, to use pension funds except for covered employees.[74]

"I sympathize with them," said Gene Orza, then the union's lawyer, "but the current players have no duty to bargain over retired employees. And you can't ask the players or the owners to give them charity. It seems unseemly."[75]

Unseemly? Cast in the light of the owners' executive council vote six months later, in January 1997, when baseball agreed to confer as charitable donations payments to the Negro Leaguers, Orza's statement is both outrageous and ironic.

No, getting a pension didn't seem unseemly to Dolph Camilli, the National League's Most Valuable Player in 1941. When asked to comment about the matter in 1996, Camilli answered, "In baseball today, you can sit on the bench for one day and get a pension." He said further, "How in the hell can they do that and not give it to people who deserve it?

---

[72] Peter King, "Hard Times for the Forgotten; Should Today's Players Help Poor Old-Timers?" *Chicago Sun Times*, August 17, 1986.

[73] Dave Anderson, "Sports of the Times; 77 Worthy Old-Timers Are Only Receiving a Major League Snub," *New York Times*, July 7, 1996.

[74] Ibid.

[75] Ibid.

"Some current player made the remark that we shouldn't be looking for a handout," Camilli continued. "They're the ones who got the handout. We set the table for them."[76]

No less than Pappas himself championed the cause of the pre-1947 players. "The players can't wait forever for someone connected with Major League Baseball to do the right thing," he wrote in the summer 1996 issue of *Outside the Lines*, the news-letter of the SABR Business of Baseball Committee.

With all due respect to the dead, this is where Pappas proved himself a hypocrite. After all, hadn't he called all the pre-1980, non-vested players "mediocrities"? What was the difference between the pre-1980, non-vested player and the pre-1947 player, anyway?

To some, the answer was nothing, except that Pappas's great-uncle, Joe Cascarella, was part of the affected class of pre-1947 players. A pitcher who toiled in both the American and National Leagues, Cascarella's best season had been in 1934, when he won 12 games for the Philadelphia Athletics.

Of the pre-1947 group, the player who was by far the most vocal about how he felt MLB and the union was cheating him out of a pension was former Brooklyn Dodger second baseman Pete Coscarart, who was named to the National League All-Star team in 1940 and who played nine seasons in the majors as a second baseman and shortstop. "The ballplayers are money-hungry, just like the owners," said Coscarart in 1997. "In my day, you were lucky you had a job."[77]

Coscarart, who wound up becoming a scout for the Minnesota Twins and the New York Yankees once his playing days

---

[76] Dwight Chapin, "After Years of Neglect, Old-Timers Sue Baseball For Unpaid Fees," *San Francisco Examiner*, August 7, 1996.
[77] Mark Hyman, "Old-Timers Take A Swing At Baseball," *Business Week*, June 9, 1997.

ended, had a reason to feel the way he did. As a member of the Pittsburgh Pirates, he strongly supported efforts in 1946 to form a players' union that could negotiate pension benefits. However, after being one of the few players who voted to support a player strike that year, he found himself out of the big leagues, sold by the Pirates to the San Diego franchise of the Pacific Coast League.

Coscarart wasn't just annoyed that he didn't receive a pension from MLB. Together with Camilli, ex-Yankees shortstop Frank Crosetti and a number of other former stars, Coscarart was the lead plaintiff in a class action suit filed in March 1996 against the league in California Superior Court alleging that baseball misappropriated the rights of publicity by using the players' names and likenesses for merchandise without their permission or proper compensation.[78]

Coscarart was also the central figure in another class action suit filed the same year contending that MLB had breached its contract with about 400 players by depriving them of pooled royalties due from the sales of products bearing their names and likenesses.[79]

"When Pete and Dolph came to me, they were really angry about the whole pension thing," recalled intellectual property attorney Ronald S. Katz, who was with the firm of Coudert Brothers 12 years ago. Now with the national law and consulting firm of Manatt, Phelps & Phillips, LLP, Katz was the attorney who filed the suit against Major League Baseball Properties, the licensing arm of MLB. "I only hope they're each now collecting a pension somewhere in heaven."

---

[78] Dwight Chapin, "After Years of Neglect, Old-Timers Sue Baseball For Unpaid Fees," *San Francisco Examiner*, August 7, 1996.

[79] Ibid.

Widely regarded as a brilliant advocate for his clients, even Katz could not get Coscarart and the rest of the players the redress they sought. In the publicity suit, a California appeals court ruled against the players in December 2001. He only fared slightly better in the second case; after a two week trial in the spring of 1998, a jury awarded the 384 old-timers seeking a greater share of MLB's licensing monies $58,000 plus interest. The verdict amounted to $151 for each player named in the suit.

Ironically, like Acho, Katz has obtained better results working on behalf of wronged football players. In November 2008, a federal jury returned a verdict against the National Football League Players Association in the staggering amount of $28.1 million, including $21 million in punitive damages, in favor of the more than 2,000 retired gridiron greats whom Katz represented who were critical of the football union's handling of its own licensing revenue. In June 2009, following an appeal by the football players association, that verdict was reduced to $26.25 million.

Sadly, as events unfolded, the fates would prove even crueler to Coscarart with regards to his long-standing attempts to receive a pension from the game he so dearly loved.

In October 1997, largely as a result of the efforts of a former minor league owner named Rick Grottanelli, a multi-millionaire who owned the now defunct Class A East Chicago Conquistadores and also used to serve as president of the independent Mid-South Professional Baseball League, MLB finally changed its tune, and decided to award all the pre-1947 players who played at least five years quarterly payments of $2,500 each.

Grottanelli's role in the resolution of the matter has all the elements of a made-for-television movie of the week. One of those larger-than-life characters you always read about, but rarely meet, the former University of Colorado All-American linebacker and centerfielder had made his millions when he had the good sense to sell the advertising and consulting business he founded in Denver to Ernst & Young, which later became the international accounting and consulting firm Ernst &Whinney.

Afterwards, because his wife's parents were ill, Grottanelli moved with her to Mississippi in order to be closer to them. While there, he hit on the idea to market and franchise all-night indoor golf courses that were open from 11 p.m. to 7 a.m. Like old-time billiard parlors and pool halls, the idea caught on, and Grottanelli made even more money for himself as a result of his stake in the company, which he called Just Puttin' Around.

Possessing an insatiable love for all sports, Grottanelli once even attempted to start a basketball league for players 6 feet 4 inches or shorter. When asked why he would risk his monies on such a venture, he answered matter-of-factly. "Ego," he said. "I want to be known for starting a league."[80]

While the temptation would be to ascribe a certain messianic complex or, at the very least, a level of self-importance to that comment, Grottanelli maintained he is not a self-centered or selfish person. Instead, he said he has a responsibility to help people because of his wealth.

"I've always had a knack for being in the right place at the right time," he adds. So, when he purchased the Conquistadores, the hands-on Grottanelli felt it was necessary to move to Valparaiso, Indiana to be closer to his team, which played at E.J. Block Stadium in East Chicago, Indiana.

---

[80] "Selling A Dream: Hoop or Pipe," *Indianapolis Post Tribune*, May 11, 1996.

And that's how he met Harry the Horse.

A four-time All-Star catcher who played for the New York Giants during his entire career, from 1933 through 1942, Harry Danning was supposedly nicknamed after the Damon Runyon character from *Guys & Dolls*. However, his daughter, Vicky Voller, who still resides in Valparaiso, offers another explanation.

"Dad used to joke he either worked like a horse or he had a face like one," she said in the fall of 2009.

A born raconteur, the elder Danning took an instant liking to the young minor league owner once Grottanelli hit town. The pair developed a deep and profound friendship that ended only when Danning passed away, in November 2004, at the age of 93.

Given his appreciation for baseball history and trivia, Grottanelli says he was enthralled by Danning's stories. "Harry was like a radio you couldn't turn off," he said. "He gave me hours of pleasure, and my memories of him are irreplaceable. I just hope I gave him as much joy as he gave me."

Their closeness and mutual respect for one another was so great that, when Grottanelli learned that Danning had lost the championship ring he had earned in 1933, when he played on the Giants team that defeated the Washington Senators in that season's World Series, Grottanelli called up the company that made the ring and had a replacement one issued to his friend at his own cost.

Similarly, when Grottanelli and his wife, Pamela, needed to rush to the airport to board an early morning plane to fly to China, where their daughter, Serafina, was born in that country's Hunan Province 13 years ago, it was none other than the then-octogenarian Danning who made sure the soon-to-be parents didn't miss their flight.

"I must be a good friend of yours," Grottanelli says Danning told him when he picked the couple up in his car. "I wouldn't get up at 4 o'clock in the morning for just anyone, you know."

So, when Danning told him that all the pre-1947 players weren't receiving pensions, it was only a matter of time before Grottanelli started making calls on behalf of Harry the Horse and Company.

One of the first people Grottanelli says he reached out to was the late Buffalo Bills and New England Patriots football coach Lou Saban. How did he know Saban? Seems that, while growing up in Hamburg, New York, where his father was principal of the local high school, Grottanelli found himself in the same third-grade class as Saban's son, Tom. Thus was born a lifelong friendship between the Saban and Grottanelli clans that still exists to this very day.

Why did he reach out to his good friend's father? When the elder Saban was the football coach at Northwestern University, he hired in 1955 a largely unknown candidate to be his receivers' coach. A man who was so personally indebted to him that, more than a quarter of a century later, he would return the favor and hire his former mentor to serve as president of his own ball club.

The ball club was the New York Yankees, and the man was George Steinbrenner.

Say what you want, though history might remember The Boss—Steinbrenner, not Bruce Springsteen—as one of the most despised and/or beloved owners in the history of the game, it is indisputable that he fielded winning teams. Perhaps not as well known, however, was the fact that Steinbrenner was extremely moved by the plight of the pre-1947 players.

"I'm an old-timer," he told CNN's Brian Jenkins in October 1996, "and having watched many of the players that were such an important part of my growing up, who are probably in the category you're talking about, I am very sympathetic to that."[81]

Even then-Yankee Darryl Strawberry, arguably one of the most self-absorbed, albeit talented ballplayers ever to put on a uniform, sided with the pre-1947 players. "A lot of people don't understand the game of baseball, and how hard players work to get to this point," he said during the same CNN interview. "They truly deserve to be treated fair in this whole situation."[82]

Grottanelli says that, because Steinbrenner had Selig's ear, his own calls to the commissioner's office were always returned.

According to his calculations, Grottanelli estimates he spent nearly $800,000 of his own money lobbying both the owners and the union on behalf of the pre-1947 players. The end result, he says, was well worth the investment.

"I love the game and these players were getting older, not younger," Grottanelli says of the reasons why he intervened to help Danning and the other men. "The bottom line was I believed I was doing something right and that justice was being served."

Grottanelli's actions didn't tip the scales of justice for Coscarart, however. For years, the old Dodger rejected the payments because, as his friend and adviser, John Puttock, of Huntington Beach, California explains, "Pete felt it wasn't really a pension. The payments would stop at his death, and he wanted to ensure that his family was protected and provided for after he passed away."

---

[81] Brian Jenkins, "Old-time Major Leaguer Fights For Pension," CNN, October 21, 1996.
[82] Ibid.

Katz agrees with Puttock. "My recollection is that these were guilt payments from MLB and not what you would characterize as true benefit allowances."

Puttock, whose boyhood hero growing up was Hall of Fame catcher Roy Campanella, founded The Campanella Society as well as a group called the Forgotten Heroes Foundation, which was formed to raise money to help the pre-1947 players, many of whom were living in genuine despair and impoverishment. As a result, Puttock grew close to a number of ex-big leaguers who played for the Dodgers while they were still based in Brooklyn, including Coscarart. To this day, he is still disappointed that Branch Rickey, the Dodgers executive most responsible for signing Robinson, "didn't stand up for Pete."

One person who did stand up for Coscarart was Sam Jethroe, the 1950 National League Rookie of the Year and former Negro League standout. When he won the coveted award, Jethroe hit .273 with 18 home runs and 100 runs scored and also swiped 35 bases for the Braves.[83]

Jethroe may have won rookie honors that year but he certainly wasn't a young man. He debuted in The Show at the age of 32 and spent a total of three years and 17 days playing for the Boston Braves and Pittsburgh Pirates.

Short of the four years he needed at that time to qualify for a pension, Jethroe brought a federal lawsuit against baseball owners, claiming discrimination left him short of the service credit he needed to be eligible for a pension.[84] Though Jethroe's suit was dismissed in October 1996, many pundits are of the opinion that it

---

[83] "Negro Leaguers Get Pensions," *New Pittsburgh Courier*, February 1, 1997.
[84] Ibid.

helped pave the way for the owners' decision the following January to award the Negro Leaguers their $10,000 payments.[85]

Given his own experiences, therefore, it wasn't a complete surprise to find Jethroe outside Dodger Stadium one hot summer evening in June 1998, lending his support to the protest that Puttock had arranged to draw attention to the plight of Coscarart and other players.[86] "I grew up in the 1960s, during the Vietnam War, when it was fashionable to hold demonstrations," said Puttock more than a decade later. Now age 60, the lawyer for a Japanese insurance company said he brought his then 14-year-old sons to the protest "to teach them that it's important to always stand up for what you believe in.

"Elderly people in this country are constantly being discriminated against," he added. "They're always shunned because they don't have much power. Well, I just thought it was great, seeing Sam and Pete together like that, marching for the same cause."

After having two heart attacks, Coscarart at long last decided to swallow his pride and take MLB up on its offer to pay him something. Call it a disbursement, call it a reparation, call it a guilt payment, call it what you will, the sick and frail Coscarart was in no position to dicker. But in a final twist, Coscarart was informed that he was not entitled to any monies because of his then still pending publicity litigation against major league baseball.

Coscarart died in July 2002 after suffering an aneurysm.

Puttock is still disgusted by baseball's handling of the Coscarart case, and points to a "Real Sports with Bryant Gumbel" episode that aired on HBO on September 15, 1998, as proof of just

---

[85] Ibid.
[86] Martha Bellisle, "Old-Time Dodgers Protest for Pension Rights," *Associated Press,* June 29, 1998.

how petty MLB can be. In the segment, entitled "Baseball Orphans," correspondent Jim Lampley told the tales of both Coscarart and ex-St. Louis Cardinals pitcher Max Lanier who, over a 14-season career, posted a more than respectable mark of 108-82 and a 3.01 ERA. Lanier, who had 21 shutouts to his credit, also hurled 91 complete games.

The father of Hal Lanier, who managed the Houston Astros to a division title in 1986, Max Lanier had already played in the bigs for six or seven seasons when he defected and joined the Mexican League in 1946 after being offered a salary nearly double what he was making with the Cardinals, according to Puttock. Disappointed by poor playing conditions and allegedly broken contract promises, he tried to return to the Cardinals in 1948, but was barred by Chandler, who had imposed a lifetime suspension on all players who had jumped to the Mexican League.

In response, Lanier sued Major League Baseball in federal court, but dropped the suit when Chandler lifted the suspension in June 1949. After rejoining the Cardinals in 1949, Lanier ended his career with the New York Giants and the St. Louis Browns.

"So he got reinstated," said Puttock, "but all his years of prior service were never credited by MLB." As a result, Lanier would sue baseball a second time, reportedly settling for $30,000 in 1998.[87]

"That's what the television show pointed out, that MLB always seems to pick the cheapest way to solve its problems," said Puttock. "I suppose they value their coffers more than fairness."

---

[87] Bill Swank, "Strike Out," *The National Pastime*, January 1, 2000.

CHAPTER 5

Shortly after the third game of the 2006 World Series, when the current CBA was agreed upon, Fehr sent both Brooks Robinson and Foster, the two executive officers of the alumni association, a cheery letter informing them of all the positive things the union had made sure to negotiate for their rank and file. Only in its third-to-last paragraph does the November 14th correspondence even address the pre-1980, non-vested player:

"Finally, from time to time you have inquired about the status of inactive, non-vested players, i.e., players who accumulated a total of less than four years of service and who had no service after the 1979 season," writes Fehr. "As you know, the subject of improvements in retirement benefits for former employees is generally not considered to be a mandatory subject of bargaining; that is, the employer is generally not required to bargain about such matters with the union, and the union may not engage in concerted action—a strike—in support of a proposal. In this case, as in previous rounds of bargaining over the benefit plan, the

Clubs were willing to agree to improvements for former players who are vested members of the Plan, but not for individuals who did not vest."

Fehr's letter is interesting because it suggests that the owners will negotiate only over vested members, rather than non-vested members. However, it also doesn't explain why the MLBPA wasn't going out on a limb for the ballplayers in question. His disingenuousness echoed a letter he penned to Neibauer nearly 15 years earlier, on January 22, 1992, when he was serving as counsel of the union:

"While we have been successful in obtaining many other improvements with respect to the Pension Plan, a reduction in the four year vesting requirement for individuals who did not have service after 1979 has not yet been achieved. Perhaps it will in future negotiations, although that is problematical in today's economic climate.

"I understand your frustration, and I hope you will also understand that current players have successfully improved pension benefits for former players in virtually every negotiation, although that has not been accomplished for individuals who never vested under the Plan," he continued. "We will have to see what future negotiations bring."

Obviously, they didn't bring Neibauer or any of the other pre-1980, non-vested players the redress they were seeking.

Rogers, the former Expo great who currently works as the liaison to the players on all things pension-related, borrowed from the same union playbook when, in answer to a reporter's question about what the MLBPA was doing to assist these men, indicated that the union recognized its obligation to past players.

"There are now guys from the 1950s and 1960s who are earning benefits that are five or 10 times higher than what they earned while they were playing," Rogers told the *Los Angeles Times* in 2007. "Each time we negotiate, we try to reach back a minimum of 10 years to get current benefits extended back in time."[88]

Rogers' intimation was clear: don't blame MLBPA for the plight of the pre-1980, non-vested player. If you want to point fingers, the blame for not helping them falls squarely on the shoulders of the owners.

In light of the fact that the MLBPA does not owe the pre-1980, non-vested players "the duty of fair representation," the union's public pronouncements on this matter are masterstrokes. Again, because of the National Labor Relations Act, it is not the current players' responsibility to negotiate on behalf of the men who came before them.

Which begets the logical question—does the players association even want to help these men?

The answer is, it depends on for whom you think unions are supposed to be working.

"The common bond that unites all unions is that they are supposed to look after their dues paying members," says Daniel R. Marburger, an associate professor of Economics at Arkansas State University who edited *Stee-rike Four! What's Wrong with the Business of Baseball* (Praeger Publishers). "The rank and file in labor unions want to make as much money for themselves as possible, even if it's at the expense of the exploited."

On the other hand, there are those who subscribe to The Three Musketeers' rallying cry—all for one and one for all. "The

[88] Greg Johnson, "Systems of Checks and Imbalances," *Los Angeles Times*, February 27, 2007.

soul of unionism, whether we're talking coal miners in the 19th century, janitors today or NBA players, is solidarity," says University of California professor Harley Shaiken. "You are working together to improve everyone's position."[89]

"Current players should continue to fight for greater retirement and health benefits for former athletes, not just for recent retirees," agrees Marc Eisenberg, author of the popular *Money Players Blog*. "All professional athletes should keep in mind that they will be active, voting members of the players association for just a few years, but they will be retired players for decades. Reaching back to improve pension benefits of retired players, particularly those who literally sacrificed their bodies to help build professional sports into a multi-billion dollar enterprise, is simply good business.

"These guys sacrificed their bodies—and in some instances, sadly, their minds—to make the league what it is today," Eisenberg continued. "They stood together through often very troubled labor negotiations, even striking on several occasions in order to improve wages and benefits not just for them, but for every player who followed. Fighting for former players sets an important precedent for future generations of professional athletes: Players take care of their own."[90]

No less than Marvin Miller, the brilliant labor economist widely credited with turning the MLBPA into a force to be reckoned with, when he was hired as its first executive director in 1966, was adamant that union members always recognize and appreciate the efforts of retired ballplayers. In an interview published in the *Los Angeles Times* in 2007, Miller said that he constantly reminded

[89] Ibid.
[90] Marc Eisenberg, "Pension Benefits For Retired Pro Athletes," *Money Players Blog*, March 1, 2007.

younger players of the need to care for past generations. During the 1960s, he would reportedly invite the widows of former baseball greats to speak to young players about their daily struggle to make ends meet.[91]

"Along with creating self-interest, I wanted to establish an ironclad precedent that this is what you do—you take care of older people who came before you," said Miller in the article.[92]

If that was really how Miller felt in 2007, you wouldn't have known it from the interview that Brown, the sports analyst from the Business of Sports Network, conducted with him three years earlier.

Asked whether he had any regrets that baseball's pension plan didn't include all those former players who hadn't met the vesting requirements, Miller expressed an entirely different point of view. "The employer, if anybody, is responsible for the pensionless status of its former employees, not the current employees," said Miller. "The employer is responsible."[93]

Even before the interview with Brown, Miller had said the exact same thing in an article written four years earlier by Bill Swank. "The employer is the supplier of pensions," he maintained. "The notion that somehow the responsibility should shift to the players is absurd. Sportswriters bought this, too. I recall talking to reporters and asking if they felt responsible for the former writers of their publications, writers of thirty, forty years ago, whom they never met. The unanimous response was that they felt no obliga-

---

[91] Johnson, "Systems of Checks and Imbalances," *Los Angeles Times*, February 27, 2007.
[92] Ibid.
[93] Marvin Miller interview, Society for American Baseball Research, Business of Baseball Committee website, July 13, 2004.

tion to pay for pensions for their predecessors since they were not the employer."[94]

Miller's assertion is yet another example of a union leader putting the onus on the baseball owners for failing to help the non-vested players.

A jaded person might argue that Fehr, Miller and Rogers have all shirked their responsibilities to the pre-1980, non-vested player. After all, more than any other issue, pensions were the reason why the players association was formed in the first place. Established in 1954, the players and owners hammered out a deal stipulating that 60% of all the revenue from the All Star Game and World Series would go to finance the players' pension fund.[95]

Fact is, player pensions was the reason for the strike that caused the delay of the start of the 1972 baseball season. All told, 86 games had to be cancelled until the season finally opened on April 15th of that year. However, by the time 1980 spring training rolled around, it was another issue entirely that had players and owners feuding like the Hatfields and McCoys.

In his superb 2002 study of the players association, *The End of Baseball As We Knew It; The Players Union, 1960-81* (University of Illinois Press), Charles P. Korr, a former professor of history at the University of Missouri at St. Louis, notes that, by the time the owners' players' relations committee formally advised the players' union, on October 30, 1979, that it intended to terminate the 1976 CBA, on December 31st of that year, which it was contractually

[94] Bill Swank, "Strike Out," *The National Pastime*, January 1, 2000.
[95] Andrew S. Zimbalist, *Baseball and Billions: A Probing Look Inside the Big Business of Our National Pastime*, Basic Books, 1992, p. 17.

obligated to do, the issue of direct compensation, rather than pensions, had become their hot button topic.[96]

According to Korr, if a team signed a free-agent in the off season who was determined to be a "quality free agent," it would have to provide his former club with another major leaguer of comparable value.[97]

In conducting his research for his book, Korr was given unparalleled access to the files of the players association. So was he ever able to unearth anything in those records about the pre-1980, non-vested ballplayer? Regrettably, when asked whether or not the topic was on anyone's radar at that time, Korr couldn't say it was or wasn't.

"Ten years have passed since I did my research," he said. "I just don't remember it being an important issue back then."

As far as the negotiations between the two sides, historian Robert F. Burk writes that the owners' negotiator, Ray Grebey, utilized what he referred to as stalking horses in dealing with the players union and Miller in 1980.[98] According to Burk, these pseudo proposals included a salary scale on pre-free agent players and the elimination of salary arbitration.[99]

What was the purpose of such ruses? Burk explains that Grebey's main objective was to boost free agent compensation. His plan required each club that signed a top tier free agent to compensate the loser by swapping it a major leaguer. Each club would be allowed to protect 15 players from this fate.[100]

[96] Charles P. Korr, *The End of Baseball As We Knew It; The Players Union, 1960-81*, University of Illinois Press, 2002, p. 190.
[97] Ibid., p. 193.
[98] Robert F. Burk, *Much More Than A Game: Players, Owners and American Baseball Since 1921*, University of North Carolina Press, 2001, p. 222.
[99] Ibid., p. 223.
[100] Ibid.

Grebey also demanded provisions requiring arbitrators to base pay rulings on players' seniority, continues Burk, and insisted on barring multiyear pacts to players with four years' or less big league service. In exchange, he offered to make anyone in the future with major league experience eligible for the pension.[101]

According to Burk, Miller feared that Grebey's proposal for immediate pension eligibility was a gambit intended to divide the union by currying favor with younger players not eligible for free agency. Consequently, he was more open to an alternative compensation idea of additional monetary payments to teams losing free agents.[102]

Whether Miller agreed to soften his position on the matter of direct compensation because he feared a divided union is beside the point. The players were now eligible for health benefits after only one day of service and a pension after 43 days—roughly one-quarter of a season.

According to Mike Marshall, the winner of the National League Cy Young Award in 1974, Miller was notorious for deliberately withholding information from player representatives such as himself.

"Marvin didn't always tell players everything we should have been told," said Marshall, who now runs his own baseball pitching and research training center in Zephyrhills, Florida. "Players were often treated like children."

Admittedly, the 66-year-old Marshall doesn't recall whether Miller during the 1980 strike negotiations properly explained to the player representatives what would occur once they voted in

---

[101] Ibid.
[102] Ibid., p. 224.

favor of amending the vesting requirement, specifically, what the impact would be on all those ex-big leaguers. "They should have gotten their years in when they were playing," said Marshall when contacted by the author in early November 2009. "But I can understand how they must feel and I certainly have sympathy for them."

Yeah, but you also have something they haven't got, Mike—a pension.

By the end of March 1980, with negotiations between the players association and the owners headed nowhere, the parties agreed to accept the services of Kenneth Moffett, a mediator from the Federal Mediation and Conciliation Service.[103]

The key issue yet to be resolved was the number of players that a club could protect from being selected as compensation for free-agent signings. Although the union seemed willing to accept a penalty of additional compensation for free agents, it adamantly opposed the owners' position of protecting only fifteen players. Protection of thirty players on the forty-man roster would have been more acceptable to the players.[104]

With negotiations seemingly at a hopeless impasse, on April 1, 1980, the MLBPA voted to cancel the remaining 92 spring training games that year but agreed to return for the start of the season and also set a subsequent strike date for May 22, which was close to the three-day Memorial Day weekend.[105]

On this point, Marshall's memory is vastly improved, if only because he contends the players' union leaked to the press that the

---

[103] Robert C. Berry, William B. Gould IV and Paul D. Staudohar, *Labor Relations in Professional Sports*, Auburn House Publishing Company, 1986, p. 65.

[104] Ibid., p. 65

[105] Kenneth Jennings, *Balls and Strikes; The Money Game in Professional Baseball*, Praeger Publishers, 1990, p. 46.

idea to cancel the remaining spring training games and come back to start the season was entirely his.

According to Kenneth Jennings, of the University of North Florida, the union's rationale was curious, to say the least. While striking during the end of spring training wouldn't represent a financial hardship to the players, and though owners probably would lose some revenues on account of cancelled exhibition games, they would likely lose more during the first week of the regular season.[106]

Still more curious was the fact that both sides failed even to meet at the bargaining table for three weeks—from April 16 thru May 6.[107] Ultimately, the strike was averted the day before the players were supposed to walk out.

"You trust the people you put in charge of a union to do what's right for you and then they don't look after your best interests," said Marshall. "Whatever we won in 1980 was of little or no benefit to me whatsoever."

Besides the new pension vesting requirements, the terms of the agreement were as follows: the minimum salary would increase to $30,000 in 1980, then $32,500, $33,500 and $35,000 over the three remaining years of the pact. The owners would contribute $15.5 million a year to the pension fund. The players association lost its proposal for reducing the amount of regular season games to be played, but was successful in reducing the eligibility for salary arbitration from three baseball seasons to two.[108]

---

[106] Ibid.
[107] Ibid., p. 47.
[108] Jennings, *Swings & Misses; Moribund Labor Relations in Professional Baseball*, Praeger Publishers, 1997, p. 5.

While the venerable *Time* took a fairly even-handed approach in its coverage of the strike that never was—the magazine's June 2, 1980 issue carried a sports item entitled "Clutch Compromise in the Ninth"—other media accounts suggested that the ballplayers cleaned the owners' clock. For example, the headline for Mike Litwin's May 20, 1980 article in the *Los Angeles Times* summed it up pretty neatly: "Owners Backed Down, Giving Miller and Players Another Victory."

Even the *Toledo Blade* got into the act: Tom Loomis' column in the paper's May 25, 1980 issue was headlined "Bluff Called, Players Win Big."

Truth be told, there really wasn't any winner. *Both* sides lost, if only because the nuclear issue of direct compensation was put on hold until the end of the year, when a four-person committee (two players and two owner representatives) charged with studying the thorny matter would present the results of its review.

With the preeminent issue still looming over both sides like a dark cloud, what had really been accomplished? Of course, the real head-scratcher was the following: why weren't men like Qualls, Fanzone, Wright, and Hutto just included retroactively when the vesting requirement was changed?

A glimpse into Fehr's views on why it wasn't possible to amend the vesting requirement retroactively could be gleaned in 2000, when he was questioned about the pre-1947 players for an article published in *The National Pastime*. Like the lawyer he is, Fehr linked their situation to that of the pre-1980, non-vested players by answering a question with a question.

"If the pre-'47 players get a pension, it raises the question, what do you do with everybody else?" he asked. "Up until 1980, it took four years to be vested. Do members from 1947 to 1979 (with less than four years in the major leagues) have priority? They played during a period covered by the pension and the pre-'47 players did not. They were members of the Players Association and the pre-'47 players were not."[109]

Nine years later, on the first Friday in November 2009, Fehr told the author during a brief phone interview that, in every subsequent collective bargaining negotiation held since 1980, the union always raised the issue about the pre-1980, non-vested players. "It's been the league that has always kept saying no," he emphasized.

Asked whether he had any remorse that the union's acceptance of instant pension eligibility in 1980 cost the affected ballplayers a chance at pensions, due to the fact that the vesting requirement was never retroactively amended, Fehr expressed disdain for the question he was posed.

"I find what you just said to me to be very strange, the way you phrased that question was very strange," he responded.

The author asked him to elaborate. What was so strange about the question?

"Let me explain something to you," Fehr told the author, completely avoiding the follow-up question. "What happened to these ballplayers was not the union's fault, okay? The union is not to blame here. The union didn't cause anything to happen.

"The owners made us a proposal for immediate pension eligibility going forward," he continued. "They are not required to negotiate over non-vested players, and we couldn't strike or threaten to strike over it. They did not make a proposal going

---

[109] Bill Swank, "Strike Out," *The National Pastime*, January 1, 2000.

backward, and for the sake of our members, we accepted it going forward, it's that simple."

Fehr, who was reportedly scheduled to receive an $11 million compensation package from the players association when he officially passed the union baton to Weiner,[110] then suggested it would be more appropriate if the author directed all future questions to his successor or, in the alternative, MLB's Manfred.

Though Fehr reportedly earned $1 million a year from 2001-2008, his salary paled in comparison to Selig, who makes $18 million a year, according to the same published account.[111]

When asked about Fehr's compensation, Curtis Granderson, the New York Yankees' All-Star outfielder who was formerly the Detroit Tigers' players representative, conceded that, while some players were concerned about the size of the package, as soon as the union membership learned "how much Bud Selig makes and we looked at how much Don Fehr hasn't made…. I think the overwhelming majority voted in favor of it."[112]

As for Fehr's predecessor, when questioned for the same *National Pastime* article, Miller answered that pension plans cannot be amended arbitrarily. "There are federal statutes preventing discrimination," he continued. "The pension plan began on April 1, 1947. You cannot arbitrarily adjust a pension plan, even if the employer agrees to bring into pension coverage the pre- '47 people, unless you bring in the post- '47 people."[113]

It makes sense, if you think it out slowly.[114] In essence, both Fehr and Miller were maintaining that the union couldn't retro-

[110] Amy K. Nelson, "Fehr Receives $11 Million Package," *ESPN.com*, October 20, 2009.
[111] Ibid.
[112] Ibid.
[113] Swank, "Strike Out," *The National Pastime*, January 1, 2000.
[114] Neil Simon, *Biloxi Blues*, Emanuel Azenberg & Center Theatre Group, Producers, 1985.

actively amend the vesting requirement for the pre-1947 players unless it amended the vesting requirements for the pre-1980 players as well.

Nearly three decades after the fact, Wright claims that the late Mark Belanger, the slick fielding shortstop of the Baltimore Orioles who was a key member of the union's executive council at that time, explained that the decision was totally random. "I think he said at some point that, 'Well, there had to be a cutoff somewhere,' and we were the ones who got screwed."

Another possible explanation for why these players were not included retroactively was that, after crunching the numbers and reviewing actuarial charts, both the union and MLB may have felt that extra benefit allowances would be too much to disburse over a long period of time. Though 874 of the pre-1980, non-vested players are still with us today, that number is down from the nearly 1,400 men who were alive in 2000.

While both explanations seem plausible, Marburger says they miss the mark entirely.

"It all comes down to one basic economic truth," he says. "Management is just not in the habit of voluntarily offering retirement benefits to people who aren't vested in pension plans."

CHAPTER 6

On Thursday, October 8, 2009, at approximately 9:15 p.m. Eastern Standard Time, the Los Angeles Dodgers' Mark Loretta lined a pitch thrown by the St. Louis Cardinals' Ryan Franklin just in front of centerfielder Colby Rasmus for a game-winning, walk-off single. The hit gave the Dodgers a commanding 2-0 lead in the best-of-five National League divisional series the two teams were playing during baseball's post-season tournament that year.

"This is the biggest hit of my career," said Loretta afterwards. "I've only played in one postseason (2005 with San Diego), and we were three and out (against the Cardinals).

"The more times you play, you savor being in these positions. (They) don't come along very often."[115]

Chances are, if you follow baseball on a regular basis, you know that Loretta had enjoyed a solid, if not spectacular career, up until that point. A resident of San Diego who, like Colbern, is a native of Santa Monica, Loretta was a two-time All-Star when

---

[115] Rick Hummel, "Loretta and Belliard Relish Their Big Hits," *St. Louis Post Dispatch*, October 9, 2009.

he signed a one-year contract with the Dodgers as a free agent in December 2008.

(Since the Dodgers did not reward Loretta for his heroics, he spent the 2009 off-season as an unsigned free agent before deciding to retire and, as this publication went to press, in January 2010, he joined the San Diego Padres as a special assistant to the team's baseball operations staff.)

In an MLB report announcing the signing, Dodgers general manager Ned Colletti was quoted as saying that Loretta "is a winning-type player. His versatility, his understanding of the game, how to prepare. That's why he's here." He added that he was looking to Loretta to provide leadership.[116]

The remaining pre-1980, non-vested ballplayers could probably say the same thing because, while he was obviously a very talented athlete, what is not as well known is that Loretta was also one of the most active player representatives in the union.

In fact, in July 2009, Loretta, who sat on the union's executive council, was selected to announce that Weiner would take over the reigns of the association from Fehr.

"Just as Major Leaguers, past and present, are very fortunate to have had Don Fehr at the helm of our union for the past 25 years, we're just as fortunate to have Michael Weiner poised and positioned to guide us into the future," said Loretta. "With more than 20 years of experience attending to virtually every aspect of union affairs, the players believe that Michael is uniquely qualified to serve as our next executive director. We're confident the full membership will agree."[117]

---

[116] Ken Gumick, "It's Official: Loretta Joins Dodgers," MLB.com, December 10, 2008.

[117] Nathaniel Vinton, "Major League Baseball Players Association Executive Board Elects Michael Weiner New Union Head," *New York Daily News*, July 9, 2009.

Six days before Loretta led the Dodgers to victory, on October 2, 2009, the players formally anointed Weiner as their new leader, by a lopsided voted of 1,055-4.

"Management is doing things right," the late management guru Peter Drucker once said. "Leadership is doing the right things."[118] By that standard, Miller and Fehr clearly did not do right by the pre-1980, non-vested players. As the final days of the summer of 2009 turned into fall, it remained to be seen whether Weiner would.

By all accounts, Weiner is a complete change of pace from Fehr, whom Grottanelli described as having "the balls of an elephant and guts of a squirrel."

The Florida business consultant wasn't singing Rogers' praises, either. "He still hasn't de-iced from when he was playing in Montreal," said Grottanelli.

Weiner, however, is a different story. "This guy is something special," said veteran baseball agent Larry Reynolds. "The guy is absolutely brilliant. And he's humble. I don't think there's anyone in the game that doesn't like Michael Weiner."[119]

"When I've had issues to be resolved and needed assistance from the other side, he's the guy I would pick up the phone and call," agreed Westhoff, the former lawyer in the commissioner's office who currently serves as a vice president of the Detroit Tigers. "He's not so dogmatic where every issue had to go to arbitration. When you try to reach an amicable settlement, he's the guy to go to. I'm very hopeful that that will translate in his new position."[120]

---

[118] Peter Drucker, *The Essential Drucker: Management, The Individual and Society*, Butterworth –Heinemann Ltd., 2001.

[119] Bob Nightengale, "No. 9; Michael Weiner, Union Counsel," *USA Today*, April 4, 2007.

[120] Alan Schwarz, "Michael Weiner, Behind-the-Scenes Force, Is Set to Move to Forefront of Major League Union," *The New York Times*, June 23, 2009.

Eddie Robinson has heard the good vibes about Weiner, as well. "I think we can work with him," he said.

Thing is, if Weiner is such a polar opposite of Fehr, who reportedly alienated fans by flaunting his intellect, even quoting ancient philosophers to make his points,[121] why hasn't the new union head ever gone to bat for the pre-1980, non-vested players before? After all, Fehr hired Weiner in 1988. Over the last two decades, hadn't he ever tried to counsel his former boss about the unfairness of this issue?

"Maybe he just wasn't in a position to do so," says Neibauer. "It's not like he was the one running the show and calling the shots."

Okay, fair enough. Hypothetically, let's say for argument's sake that Fehr believed he was running an autocracy instead of a labor union. That means either one of two things occurred when it came to the topic of the pre-1980 players—either Fehr and, to a lesser extent, Miller, never told the player representatives about this situation or, as Marburger suggests, they were told and didn't want to help the retirees because it would take money out of their own pockets.

Marburger, for one, says he could never fathom the former explanation. "It's my understanding that the players' union under his (Fehr's) leadership was a very democratic shop, that input was always solicited and that opinions were valued."

Well, then that only leaves one other alternative.

Again, federal law doesn't require current dues-paying players to bargain on behalf of non-vested players. And yes, if they were to do so, it's likely their own share of the pie wouldn't be as

---

[121] Ibid.

great. But is it likely, or even conceivable, that not one player representative over the course of the last three decades recognized that an injustice was being perpetrated on some 1,000 ex-ballplayers? An injustice that could easily be remedied by just retroactively amending the vesting requirements?

Does anyone seriously believe that Chris Capuano, the former Milwaukee Brewers players' representative, wouldn't have spoken up about this matter? A Duke University graduate who majored in economics, surely Capuano, who was attempting a comeback in September 2009 after two surgeries on his arm, would have recognized the incongruity of this situation.

And what about Doug Glanville, the former Phillie, Cub and Ranger who used to write the popular "Heading Home" column in *The New York Times*? Glanville, who still occasionally serves as an Op-Extra columnist for the *Times,* and who bills himself on his website as "The Academic Ambassador to Baseball," was a players' representative who formerly served on the union's executive council. If he wanted guidance about this issue, Glanville needed to look no farther than his own household, since his wife, Tiffany, is an associate at Miner, Barnhill & Galland, a Chicago-based firm specializing in employment and labor law.

Or how about Rick Helling, a Stanford University graduate who served as a players association executive board member for eight years, from 1999 thru 2007? A member of the union negotiation committee on the CBA while he was still an active player, Helling was hired in the spring of 2009 to be a special assistant to the MLBPA executive director. An avowed opponent of steroids during his playing days, Helling is widely acknowledged to be the player who slammed MLB for looking the other way when it came to the use of performance enhancing drugs in the big leagues.[122]

In an attempt to question Helling regarding his feelings on this matter, the author telephoned the ex-hurler at what he believed was his home in Minnesota. A woman who claimed to be Helling's mother answered the phone at the house and said she would get word to her son who, to date, has not returned the call.

Or what about Granderson, who has traveled to Italy, China and South Africa as an ambassador for Major League Baseball International? The son of two Illinois teachers, Granderson in 2008 established the Grand Kids Foundation, which focuses on the importance of educational initiatives for children and also helps to reintroduce the sport of baseball in inner cities across the country.

How is it even remotely possible that such caring, smart and thoughtful men as Capuano, Glanville, Helling and Granderson could seemingly have turned a blind eye to this issue?

One former assistant player's representative says that the inactive, non-vested, pre-1980 players ought to get something for their troubles, if only because the Negro Leaguers were awarded payments from MLB.

"You just can't give stuff away to one group and not the other," says Ron Kittle, the 1983 American League Rookie of the Year who still does occasional community and public relations work for the Chicago White Sox. "If the Negro Leaguers got a pension, these guys are deserving of it too."

Kittle's position is hardly surprising since, like Grottanelli, he had also befriended Danning. "He was sharp as a tack," recalled

---

[122] Mark Zwolinski, "Rick Helling, Mike Myers Named MLBPA Executive Director Special Assistants," *Toronto Star*, March 18, 2009.

Kittle, now a motivational speaker who established a nonprofit foundation, Indiana Sport Charities, that's dedicated to eradicating cancer, which took his father's life, "He played in some of my charity golf tournaments, and boy, did he know how to tell a good story."

So when questioned in 1996 about whether he believed the pre-1947 players ought to be awarded a pension, Kittle said Danning's predicament wasn't fair. "The old guys of the game went to bat for us," he answered. "Maybe it's time we went to bat for them."[123]

Kittle is like Clyde in that he says what he thinks. "Nobody puts me on the spot," he says. "I had a tough assed father who worked every day in the mill. I believe people in any profession who gave their all, who gave their 100 percent, are deserving of something. If these players did their job, they should get a pension."

At the same time, however, while Kittle freely acknowledges that "these guys were part of the great baseball fraternity, and they should be proud of that," he also believes that rules are rules. "I was dealt a hand and I had to play it," says Kittle, who injured his neck at age 18 and years later also wound up in the hospital after suffering a spinal injury. "So should these guys."

In essence, Kittle was exhorting the players to suck it up and move on. A big fan of Disney movies, he might as well have just quoted Jeremy Irons' opening line from *The Lion King*: "Life's not fair, is it?"[124]

---

[123] Richard Grey, "No Requiem for the Man Called Horse," *Indiana Post* Tribune, October 17, 1996.

[124] *The Lion King* (1994), Buena Vista Pictures & The Walt Disney Studios, Irene Mecchi, Jonathan Roberts & Linda Woolverton- Screenwriters.

Kittle later attempted to clarify his position regarding the pension-less players. "If they deserve it," he said of the pre-1980 group, "they should get it."[125]

At least one of the pre-1980 players feels he actually doesn't deserve an MLB pension.

"I don't want welfare, I don't want something for nothing," said former St. Louis Cardinals pitcher Dan O'Brien, who appeared in a total of 13 games over two seasons with the Redbirds, from 1978 to 1979. "If you're going to live your life for a pension, you probably didn't prepare yourself very well for retirement."

A former Academic All American at Florida State University, the 55-year-old O'Brien, who says he never earned more than $21,000 while playing baseball, took an early buyout from the Michigan public school system in 2008 after putting in 20 years as a social studies teacher at Dundee High School. A onetime assistant head coach at the University of Michigan, he is now a volunteer coach for the Eastern Michigan University baseball team.

"I was blessed that I didn't have any catastrophic injuries when I played," says O'Brien, whose brother-in-law, Bill Freehan, was the five-time Gold Glove Award-winning catcher who was selected to play in 11 All-Star Games during his entire 15-year career with the Detroit Tigers. "So I think having health insurance is equally as important as receiving a pension. But truthfully, I think the league can help players in more tangible ways."

What does he suggest? Not surprisingly, O'Brien, who holds a master's degree in counseling from Southern Illinois University, says the league ought to try to do a better job preparing its players for life after the game.

---

[125] October 9, 2009 email to the author.

"Education is everything," says O'Brien. "For guys who didn't do anything with their lives, we can do a better job helping them so they don't need welfare, we can help them find gainful employment and see to it that they're ready for life after baseball."

When asked whether MLB had any type of counseling program that helps retired ballplayers adjust to civilian life, Manfred said the league did not. "Any such program," he explained, "would have to be developed jointly with the MLBPA. The MLBPA has never made a proposal to develop such a program."[126]

"When I played, we all knew when we got to the big leagues that we had to get our four years in, so the bottom line is, why should they give me a pension?" asks O'Brien. "What did I do in the game that merits me getting one?"

Whether someone feels they *deserve* something or not is, of course, entirely subjective. But as things stand now, the reality is these players are not *entitled* to pensions.

While the candor of both Kittle and O'Brien is refreshing, they are clearly in the minority when it comes to speaking out about this matter. Regrettably, when asked whether they thought the pre-1980, non-vested ballplayers were getting the short end of the stick, the lion's share of players both past and present who were contacted for this book avoided this issue like the plague.

Take Lyle Overbay, for instance. The power hitting first baseman for the Toronto Blue Jays is a longtime friend of the Fast family, whose children play soccer with Fast's grandchildren. During the off-season, Overbay and his family regularly attend services at Darcy Fast's church. But when the pastor's son, Christian, asked his friend to consider furnishing the author

---

[126] November 19, 2009 email to the author.

124 | A BITTER CUP OF COFFEE

with a statement for attribution, he begged off, claiming he didn't know what the position of his own team's player representative was regarding this issue.

Interestingly, Christian Fast did indicate that, when he told his friend that his father wasn't receiving a pension, Overbay expressed surprise and told him it was the first time he had ever heard anything about the story of the pre-1980, non-vested players.

And then there's the curious case of Casey Candaele.

The onetime player representative of the Houston Astros, Candaele was known as quite the clubhouse comedian during his playing days. The inventor of "naked batting practice," as well as a master at "airplane skiing," which involved riding an airplane tray down the aisle of a team's charter plane, Candaele was the first major leaguer whose own mother, Helen Callaghan Candaele, had also played professional baseball.[127]

Candaele's mother played in the fabled All-American Girls Professional Baseball League (AAGPBL), and his brother, Kelly—who up until the summer of 2009 was a member of the Board of Directors of the Los Angeles City Employees' Retirement System—made a documentary about the AAGPBL that served as the inspiration for the classic Penny Marshall movie, *A League of Their Own.*

Given his brother's work, as well as his own experiences with the players association, one might reasonably expect Candaele to be able to offer some keen insights about the topic of the pre-1980, non-vested players. However, when contacted for his thoughts, Candaele issued a simple and succinct statement.

---

[127] Alyson Footer, "Where Have You Gone, Casey Candaele?" MLB.com, January 23, 2002.

"I'm not interested in talking about this topic," wrote Candaele.[128]

Jeez Casey, why don't you tell us how you really feel?

Mind you, even some of the pre-1980, non-vested players themselves preferred not to talk on the record about this issue. Rod Gaspar, who was part of the "Miracle Mets" team that beat the Orioles in the 1969 World Series—while running for Jerry Grote, who had led off the bottom of the 10th inning of Game 4 with a double, Gaspar came around to score the winning run after pinch hitter J.C. Martin bunted and pitcher Pete Richert's throw hit Martin on the wrist as he ran to first base—declined to comment, even though he would obviously stand to benefit if he and the rest of the ex-ballplayers in the group were to receive pensions.

"I don't think it's necessary," he said when the author contacted him by telephone for an interview. The 63-year-old Gaspar now sells insurance in Mission Viejo, California.

Candaele's and Gaspar's refusal to share their views on the subject is puzzling, but it pales in comparison to that of Robin Roberts.

One of the most respected men ever to play the game, Roberts is widely acknowledged to have been the driving force behind the hiring of Miller to be the union's first executive director. As the "Biography" page on his own official website, RobinRoberts36.com, proudly notes, Roberts "was instrumental in the hiring of Marvin Miller… as the head of the screening committee for the Players Association, Robin convinced the players' representatives from the individual teams that Miller was the right choice."

---

[128] October 5, 2009 email to the author.

So when the author contacted Larry Shenk, a vice president of the Philadelphia Phillies, in mid-August 2009 seeking an interview with the Hall of Fame pitcher, to learn his thoughts about what could be done to help the inactive, pre-1980, non-vested players, imagine his surprise when Shenk indicated that Roberts wasn't interested.

"I just spoke with Robbie and he prefers to pass on this request," wrote Shenk.[129]

First Bunning, then Roberts. What is it about Hall of Fame pitchers from Philadelphia, the author wondered, that they shut up like clams whenever this topic is broached?

Is Roberts willing to talk about anything? He is, but presumably you have to pay for that privilege. You'll find the following nugget if you visit the "Appearances" page of Roberts' website:

> To someone like Robin, who started in baseball in 1948 when the minimum salary was $5,000 and top players made $25,000 to $50,000, the present day salary scale is unreal. Robin is in the unique position to discuss these changes and explain his role, for example, in how Marvin Miller was chosen and the effect of having a well run players association.... Although it is more fun to talk about the games, the business side of sports has certainly become important.... Robin is available to appear before your group to talk sports and answer questions. To get more information on how to have Robin appear at your event, please contact us at *info@robinroberts36.com*.

---

[129] August 13, 2009 email to the author.

Though he might have been reluctant to speak on the record with a writer about the inactive, non-vested players, Roberts did attempt to press the issue with a number of high-level baseball officials, including Manfred, during the 2009 All-Star Game held in St. Louis.

In a July 16, 2009 memorandum sent from Foster to Clyde, Skok, Eddie Robinson and Neibauer, the alumni association executive director advised the four members of the pension subcommittee that both he and Roberts were staying at the same hotel for the game and briefly chatted about the issue on a few occasions. Had Roberts' conversations with Manfred been productive?

According to Foster, "Robin said, 'It's going to be a tough sell, Dan, a tough sell.'"

Foster wrote that he also met with Manfred at the hotel to discuss the plight of the pre-1980 players. What Manfred apparently told him was not encouraging, either.

"The facts are that the current plan assets are down significantly; they've dropped below federal guidelines for (pension) funding requirements," continued Foster. He explained that, pursuant to the terms of the current CBA, which was ratified in 2006 and which expires in December 2011, "the owners will be asked and required to increase their current annual contributions from $157 million to more than $210 million in order to cover this deficit. This makes asking for additional funds for former employees difficult."

In effect, it was Foster's opinion that Manfred was signaling there was no way that a new CBA could be written which included amending the vesting requirements for the pre-1980 players. He then indicated he suggested to Manfred that other revenue streams could be tapped that might be able to fund the inactive players' proposed pensions. Which ones did he have in mind? Specifically, Foster recommended raiding the Competitive Balance Tax (CBT).

Often referred to somewhat facetiously as the "Steinbrenner luxury tax," because of the Yankees' marked tendency to push their payroll past $100 million each season by signing free agents to lucrative, long-term contracts, the CBT is reportedly supposed to discourage high team salaries by requiring clubs to pay a penalty once a certain threshold is reached. The monies from the tax then go into an account that's later distributed to all the other ball clubs; infused with this extra capital, smaller market teams are supposed to be able to compete on a more level playing field with teams like the Yankees, thereby ensuring league parity.[130]

Only 25 percent of the CBT is actually used to grow the game, according to Foster. As an example of what he meant, he indicated that monies from the CBT pay for travels to China to expand baseball in the Far East.

In his memo to the members of the pension committee, he explained that 50 percent of the CBT is dedicated to the current players' 401k contributions, while the remaining 25 percent is supposed to be earmarked as a contingency to cover any shortfalls in the players' health plan.

According to Foster's memo, Manfred embraced the idea after the alumni leader ran it by him.

"Rob said there is a possibility that there may be excess dollars from the CBT at the end of 2011 and he could get Bud

---

[130] Darren Rovell, "Owners; Luxury Tax No Guarantee of Competitive Balance," ESPN.com, August 14, 2002.

Selig to agree to use this money for the inactive, non-vested if the union would also agree," Foster continued. "We talked about the sustainability of the dollars, and Rob said he would talk to Michael Weiner about it."

According to the memo, Manfred made it clear that this creative, out-of-the box idea—or something like it—was the perfect end around of the CBA.

Contacted in late November 2009 about his meeting with Foster in St. Louis, Manfred acknowledged that he has "had on-going conversations with Mr. Foster. At various times, I have explained that maintaining the current plan is very expensive, particularly given the developments in the investment markets in the last 18 months. Adding new participants adds to the expense. I have told Mr. Foster that Commissioner Selig is open to potential creative solutions to this problem that involve funding not only by the Clubs, but also by the players."[131]

As far as tapping into the CBT was concerned, however, Foster wrote in his memo that he met with Fehr, Weiner and Rogers the day after the All-Star game was played, on Wednesday, July 15, 2009, and that the union trio was not as enthusiastic about using the monies earmarked for the CBT to pay the pre-1980 players. According to his memo, while "they said that the intent is all well and good, there are additional commitments to the CBT" that had to be factored into the equation.

According to Foster, Fehr and Weiner instead recommended that groups of players from each team should go to their respective owners and convince each one of them to contact Selig. "(They said) it would be a great legacy for him to fund this," he wrote.

---

[131] November 19, 2009 email to the author.

Foster ended his memo by cautioning the committee not to do anything rash. "(Manfred, Fehr and Weiner) all continue to remind me that any inflammatory action at this point would have a negative impact," he told the foursome.

Upon reading the memo, Neibauer says he just laughed. "What are they going to do to me?" he remembers thinking to himself. "Take away my pension?"

Third

CHAPTER 7

In the fall of 2009, the debate over President Barack Obama's health care reform proposals took an interesting turn when members of the Fourth Estate, who had mostly treated candidate Obama with kid gloves when he was running for the White House in 2008, started assailing the administration left and right. The president's press secretary, Robert Gibbs, responded by routinely issuing denunciations of the administration's critics; in effect, Gibbs decided to fight fire with fire.

"The best analogy is probably baseball," said Gibbs. "The only way to get somebody to stop crowding the plate is to throw a fastball at them. They move."[132]

Not surprisingly, an early advocate of playing hardball with both the league and the union was Colbern, who says he's not in the habit of letting people walk all over him. A number of people interviewed by the author claimed the disgruntled former back-stop wanted to picket the 2009 All-Star Game by demonstrating

---

[132] Michael Scherer, "Calling 'Em Out," *Time Magazine*, October 19, 2009.

outside of Busch Stadium in St. Louis, but the idea was quickly killed, according to Skok.

Hutto, however, said that Dick Baney, the former pitcher for the Seattle Pilots and Cincinnati Reds, was actually the ex-player who fueled the idea of a mass protest at the All-Star Game.

When asked to set the record straight once and for all, Baney, who resides in Tustin, California, said he's the one who came up with the idea and later told Colbern about it.

"Don't get me wrong," said Baney, who was contacted by the author a week before he was set to turn 63, on November 1, 2009. "I love the game of baseball, I just don't like the way baseball has treated me and all the other guys affected by this."

"There's no incentive, no rush for the union or the league to do anything for us," agreed Baney's friend, 63-year-old Jerry Janeski. A successful realtor with First Team Estates, a luxury real estate firm representing high end buyers and sellers in Southern California, Janeski pitched a complete game shutout in his second big league appearance in 1970, when he compiled a 10-17 record for a woeful Chicago White Sox club that went 56-106 that season.

Janeski, who admits he's done very well for himself since his playing days ended, added that, while he may not need a pension as badly as men such as Colbern, Hutto or Wright, "this is about fairness, plain and simple.

"It is outlandish that people who have put their time in are not getting anything for that time," he continued. "It makes you feel insignificant, like your accomplishments and time in the game weren't meaningful." Both the league and the union, he said, need to be held accountable.

According to Baney, that's exactly what he tried to impress upon Foster. At the alumni association meeting held in Palm Springs, California in 2006, Baney said he had a one-on-one meeting with Foster and told him point blank that baseball needed to be "embarrassed."

"Baseball hates being embarrassed," he continued. "It doesn't matter whether we're talking about the stupid Acho lawsuit or (New York Yankee superstar) Alex Rodriguez's admission that he took steroids while he was with the Rangers. Baseball doesn't like controversy."

Baney, on the other hand, says he has no problem fanning the flames of controversy. "My All-Star Game idea was to hire a couple of people for minimum wage, and have them parade around in front of Busch with sandwich placards. On one side, it would read in big, bold lettering something like, 'Major League Baseball Has Turned Its Back On Players.' And then on the other side there'd be a toll-free phone number where people could call for more details."

But that's only for starters, says Baney. "We should just go and hire ourselves a real shark, somebody like discrimination attorney Gloria Allred or someone of that caliber, someone who would try to get us all grandfathered back into the CBA and who wouldn't be afraid to take on the league. That way we'd be sending a message."

At least one of the ex-players agrees with Baney. "A message definitely needs to be sent," said Hutto. "For years, all we heard in the locker rooms and in the clubhouses was how ballplayers take care of one another. Well, that's just plain bullshit, that kind of attitude doesn't exist today."

Baney says he is disappointed that the alumni association hasn't been more forceful regarding the retirees' situation. "How come the association isn't behind us? I asked Foster about this three years ago. And he says, 'Well, I'm behind you.' That's when I lost all faith in Dan Foster as a leader. I'm telling you, they (MLB) better make us some kind of serious offer soon.

"I get an alumni association solicitation in the mail telling me the group raised $13 million last year on behalf of charity, and then they've got the gall to ask me to write a check, to write a donation that will support more charitable efforts," continued Baney. "Well, who's supporting us?

Baney poses a reasonable question, especially in light of the fact that so many of the alumni weren't even aware that the group was actively doing anything on their behalf. "This is the first I've ever heard anything about it," said 62-year-old George Theodore, of Salt Lake City, Utah, when the author contacted him the night before the World Series was scheduled to begin, on October 27, 2009. "It's really disconcerting that I've never received any information about this before."

Better known to fans of the New York Mets by his nickname of "The Stork," Theodore's been the alumni association's chapter president in Utah for many years, and is quite proud of the work that his chapter does, particularly with respect to the instructional clinics the group puts on for underprivileged youngsters.

"The Mets treated me very well," said Theodore who, once his playing career ended, went back to school and earned a master's degree in social work. A social worker for the largest school district in the state, the Granite School District, for the past 32 years,

Theodore says he expects to receive a pension for his years spent counseling the future generation when he retires at the age of 65.

"I am working in a great position and I've enjoyed myself immensely," adds Theodore of his post-playing career. "But anything I'd get from my time in the game would be nice, because I live in a state that hasn't historically paid its educators well."

In spite of having the highest pupil-per-teacher ratio in the nation, Utah's teachers rank 49th in terms of average salary levels, at $37,775, according to the American Federation of Teachers.[133]

"The union should be looking out for us also," continued Theodore. "I think some of today's players should learn how to give back a bit."

His fellow Utah alum, Bruce Christensen, the onetime short-stop for the California Angels before the team rechristened itself as the Los Angeles Angels of Anaheim, agrees with The Stork. "I feel today's group should be more respectful of the game and of the players who played before them," says Christensen, who resides with his family in Moroni, Utah, a little town with just over 1,300 people in it. "There have been big changes in baseball since I first played, and one of the biggest is that the game is all about agents and money today. So I won't deny it'd be nice if we got compensated too.

"After our playing days came to an end, the transition was a big change for many of us, but I've been fortunate," continued Christensen who, like O'Brien, thinks the league can do a better job helping its players adjust to civilian life. Never at a loss for finding jobs after he left the game, Christensen says that some of the positions he held included working for a cement plant company and as a certified warrantor. "I haven't been sitting around thinking about

---

[133] *Survey and Analysis of Teacher Salary Trends, 2007*, American Federation of Teachers, 2008.

what might have been, but everyone could always use a little extra money," he said.

In their efforts to get players such as Christensen that money, the pension committee members also discussed writing to the 30 player representatives. After all, according to Foster's July 16, 2009 memo, hadn't Fehr and Weiner recommended that the players speak to their owners about this issue? The problem was, the names of each of the 30 player reps is as well guarded a secret as is the formula to Coca-Cola, which is stored in the vault of Sun Trust Bank's corporate headquarters, in Atlanta, Georgia.

While it was generally known that Loretta and Granderson were active in the players association, and that Hunter Pence, John Buck, Troy Tulowitzki and Brandon Morrow served as the player reps for, respectively, the Astros, Kansas City Royals, Colorado Rockies and Seattle Mariners, the names of the other men who were team player reps in 2009 were as mysterious as an Agatha Christie novel.

Neibauer, Hutto and Wright had also bandied about the notion of recruiting a marquee former player to act as a spokesman for the inactive, pre-1980, non-vested bunch. This approach had worked wonders for retirees in the NFL; whenever one thought about the struggles of ex-football players, the trio reasoned, people like Mike Ditka and Barney automatically came to mind, not because they were down on their luck, but because the two pigskin greats were always speaking out on behalf of those football retirees who were dealing with hardships after their own playing careers had ended.

Wright says that both he and Hutto contacted Ditka's personal secretary regarding the matter, but that the gatekeeper never relayed their messages to the coaching legend, who made the Pro Football Hall of Fame in Canton, Ohio as a tight end.

Of course, Roberts or Bunning would have been perfect for such an effort but, given their reticence to discuss this issue in public, neither man's participation or involvement was ever seriously considered.

In typical fashion, Colbern had volunteered to be the "poster boy" for the pre-1980 players, but even he conceded that he "wasn't a big enough name" to attract attention to the cause. Qualls says the late Dom DiMaggio had shown some interest in the matter, but not enough to start seriously lobbying anyone.

"It doesn't seem like anyone wants to step forward and be the poster child for us," agreed Steve Grilli, the former Detroit Tigers pitcher who now runs a popular sports bar, A Change of Pace, on Grant Boulevard in Syracuse, New York. A right-hander who pitched in a total of 70 games over parts of four seasons with the Tigers, Grilli logged a combined total of 138 innings during the 1976 and 1977 seasons.

"I spent almost one-third of my life in the game," said the 60-year-old Grilli, who scouted for the St. Louis Cardinals for six years after playing nearly 11 in the major and the minor leagues. "And I've got absolutely nothing to show for it."

The father of pitcher Jason Grilli, the Brooklyn, New York native has a deep and profound respect for the game. "Jason was the fourth pick when he was drafted in the first round by the San Francisco Giants in 1997 so what did I do? I bought him a book about the Giants so he could learn the history behind the club that had selected him, that he was now on the team that some of the real greats of the game, guys like Willie Mays, Juan Marichal and Willie McCovey, had also played for."

Grilli says he was honored and privileged to put on a big league uniform for as many years as he did, and that feeling of appreciation is what he hopes he passed onto his son who, during his own eight-year career in the big leagues, has already pitched for five clubs—the Florida Marlins, the Detroit Tigers, the Chicago White Sox, the Colorado Rockies and the Texas Rangers, as well as Team Italy during the World Baseball Classic.

"I was a non-roster invitee to the Tigers' spring training camp one year, when who do you think comes up to me? None other than Billy Martin himself pulls me over and says to me, 'Hey *paisan*, remember, this is where you want to be.'"

Rest assured, if the late "Billy the Kid" hadn't reminded him of how fortunate he was to don a baseball uniform, Grilli says there were plenty of veterans on the Tigers, including his former battery mate, Freehan, who made sure he didn't get a swelled head.

"One game, we're playing the Red Sox and I'm trying to be cute with my pitches to Carl Yastrzemski," recounts Grilli. "So Freehan comes out to the mound and really puts things in proper perspective for me. He says, 'That's Carl *friggin* Yastrzemski you're pitching to. He's a future Hall of Famer and you're not. These people came to see him hit and not to see you pitch, just remember that.'"

And of course, Grilli especially cherishes certain milestone moments. Asked about his first appearance in the majors, he has no problem whatsoever recalling who was the first batter that he ever faced.

"It was Hall of Famer Jim Rice," he quickly replies. "And wouldn't you know it, Jim Rice was also the *last batter* I ever pitched to in the big leagues, too.

"My memories, my experiences, I'd never trade anything in the world for them," continued Grilli. However, as priceless as his memories are to him, Grilli is still steamed that he's not getting a pension. "I paid union dues when I played, and now we're told that the union doesn't owe us representation," he fumed. "I'm a victim of circumstance, all because three decades ago either somebody forgot to write us into that CBA or they didn't want to write us into the contract at all.

"I feel like I'm just being swept under the carpet," Grilli continues. "You know, I didn't make a whole lot of money when I was playing, my first contract in the big leagues was for only $16,500, and that's because I played in an era when the pendulum was swung in favor of the owners." Money was so tight that Grilli says he used to siphon off gas from a used car lot just to avoid having to fill up at the pump.

Asked who he believes would be the logical choice to spearhead this campaign, Grilli without hesitation offers up the name of Brooks Robinson.

Clyde felt the same way. So, too, did Neibauer, who dashed off a June 20, 2007 letter to the president of the board of the alumni association more than 15 months before Hutto's own sharply worded correspondence to Robinson. In it, not only does Neibauer encourage Robinson to "become more active personally and publicly in supporting benefits for the almost 900 inactive, non-vested players," but reminds the human vacuum cleaner that taking a proactive approach was clearly paying huge dividends for retired NFL players.

"It is interesting to note that some of the NFL's all-time greats and Hall of Famers... have visibly and vocally joined the effort to obtain benefits for their fellow players," wrote Neibauer. "Perhaps the NFL players' approach is the alternative we need to publicize the lack of benefits for our group. It would seem that with the NFL players' efforts making news, MLBPAA would be interested in following their lead."

As Hutto would no doubt attest, Robinson must take an inordinately long time to answer his mail. That's because Neibauer is still awaiting the courtesy of a response from him, as well.

Because the idea to recruit a big name player never panned out, instead of firing fastballs, the MLBPAA pension committee members wound up extending an olive branch to both the union and the league. Informed by Foster that Manfred and Weiner had both agreed to discuss the issue at a face-to-face, sit-down meeting, to be held at MLB's Park Avenue offices in Manhattan on Thursday, October 1, 2009, Neibauer says he was convinced to withhold sending the "Raise the BAR" letter that the group had prepared over the summer.

In return, Neibauer says Foster told the committee that Manfred and Weiner also promised to jointly forward correspondence to all the affected retirees indicating that they genuinely wanted to help them.

Who asked that the letter be put on hold? Out of a sense of loyalty to his fellow committee members, Neibauer isn't divulging the name of the person who requested that the correspondence be tabled, but it doesn't take a rocket scientist to figure out who the most likely suspect was.

Right off the bat, Clyde was perhaps the easiest person to eliminate from consideration, given his past flare-ups with Fehr and Rogers and history of saying what he means and doing what he says.

That left only Skok and Eddie Robinson, and two of the retirees think the answer is obvious, albeit for different reasons.

"It's pretty apparent that Eddie's been calling in favors for us," says Colbern.

"I just don't trust Eddie," said Wright. "He's a former general manager with close ties to both Selig and Manfred."

While Wright could be right, only Neibauer knows for sure.

To his credit, Neibauer wasn't leaving anything to chance. Shortly before leaving with his family on a vacation in mid-September 2009, he picked up the phone and, with the help of an intermediary, called someone who he knew had been down this road before. Though he had never personally met him, Neibauer was nonetheless interested in speaking to Grottanelli about the plight of the pre-1980 players.

Grottanelli, who never quite got the props he deserved for intervening on behalf of the pre-1947 players, was more than happy to assist. "I think I can help them get over the humps," he told the author after speaking with Neibauer. "I think I can be an asset to them, and I believe it can be accomplished if the right steps are followed. You know, things like this do tend to rattle the foundation a bit."

Unfortunately, Rick Grottanelli never got the chance to go two for two. Less than two weeks after speaking to Neibauer, on Sunday, September 27, 2009, the generous and big-hearted business consultant died of a massive heart attack. He was 57 years old.

CHAPTER 8

Prior to the start of the inaugural Baseball Hall of Fame Classic, held on June 21, 2009 at Doubleday Field in Cooperstown, Grilli and Rogers, who were both invited to participate in the exhibition game, ran into one another. Grilli, who would surrender only one hit in his inning of work as a member of the winning "Team Wagner," asked the players association executive, who would face five batters as a member of "Team Collins," if there were any new developments to report about whether he and the rest of the pre-1980, non-vested players would ever get a pension.

"We made some small talk, and then I asked him if there was any movement, any progress, that he could tell me about," remembers Grilli. "And he looks at me and says, 'Well, you know if you guys ever get anything, it's not going to be a true pension, you understand that, right?'"

Grilli is still annoyed by what he describes as Rogers' insensitivity and callous disregard for his feelings. "I mean, what kind of answer was that? What is baseball going to do, just throw us a bone? I want a real pension."

"If they try to throw me a bone, I'm telling you right now, I'd turn it down," said Baney. "I once told Foster that I'd donate my pension back to the alumni, but you know what? Times change, people change, and after all these years, I want one now more than I ever have before. It's the principle of the thing."

The point was not lost on the individual members of the alumni association's special pension committee. "Obviously, in a perfect world, the ideal would be to just grandfather us back into pension eligibility," said Clyde. "But I don't even know if that's possible."

According to Skok, it's not, due to the "restrictions imposed by the federal government and ERISA (Employee Retirement Income Security Act) laws governing pension plans."[134]

A federal law that sets minimum standards for retirement and health benefit plans in the private sector, the Employee Retirement Income Security Act of 1974 provides that those individuals who manage plans must meet certain standards of conduct. The law also contains detailed provisions for reporting to the government and disclosure to participants. The United States Department of Labor's Employee Benefits Security Administration (EBSA), along with the Pension Benefit Guaranty Corporation and the Internal Revenue Service (IRS) of the United States Department of Treasury, is charged with seeing to it that ERISA is adhered to and complied with.

Asked whether the vesting requirements of pension plans could be retroactively amended, EBSA's chief economist and director of policy and research, Joseph Piacentini, begged off, explaining that the question would be better directed to the

---

[134] October 26, 2009 email to the author.

Department of Treasury, "which has regulatory and interpretive authority over the vesting provisions."[135]

Subsequently, an IRS spokesman indicated that federal law prohibits the IRS from disclosing any facts pertaining to individual taxpayers.[136]

When, on November 11, 2009, the author contacted the 92-year-old Miller about ERISA and how it affected the pre-1980, non-vested players, the former executive director of the players association indicated he had been misquoted in *The National Pastime* article published on January 1, 2000. "I never said anything about federal statutes and discrimination," he said. "But it is absolutely correct that you cannot arbitrarily amend a pension plan."

Though his beloved wife had passed away only 15 days earlier, Miller was gracious and polite in answering the author's questions. "I'm happy to oblige you," he said from his apartment on the Upper East Side of Manhattan. "I am quite certain a lot of people are confused about this matter. The fact is, most people don't know a lot about pension plans. What people have never understood about pension plans could fill up the New York Public Library."

Miller maintained that, under ERISA, "the assets of a pension plan belong to only the vested members of the plan, and nobody else." People who were never part of a pension plan, he added, could therefore not be introduced into the plan.

"Now, as far as I know, nobody has attempted to adjudicate this in court yet, because I think the law is pretty clear on this point," Miller continued. "But in my opinion, that would seem to be the only way these players could be restored to coverage."

---

[135] November 9, 2009 email to the author.
[136] November 19, 2009 email to the author.

Unlike Fehr, who scoffed at the author's question about whether or not he felt bad for these players' situation, Miller actually admitted he had entertained the idea of trying to change the vesting requirement. "Did I ever think of retroactively amending it? Of course I did," he said. "But the plain truth is, we weren't ever going to refuse management's offer of instant pension eligibility. That wouldn't have been in the best interests of all the members of our union back then."

Miller also agreed with Burk's assessment that Grebey's proposal was intended to divide the union. "Yes, Mr. Grebey and the owners were trying to buy us off with this one day eligibility plan, I absolutely concur with that."

Not surprisingly, Miller wasn't pleased that Marshall had accused him of withholding information from the players. "I consulted with all the players who were part of our executive council and who were on that negotiating team in 1980," he said. "I'm sorry he feels that way."

He was also sorry about one other thing. Only the day before, on November 10, 2009, Miller had learned that his name would once again be placed on the "Executives and Pioneers" ballot being considered by a 12-member veterans' committee charged with electing new members to the Baseball Hall of Fame in 2010. Miller, who was also eligible for the honor in 2003, 2007 and 2008, said that, after being rebuffed the first three times, he didn't need election to the Hall to feel good about his numerous contributions to the labor movement and to the players association.

"I've told the Hall that I don't want my name placed on the ballot, but they keep putting me on it anyway," said Miller, who was rebuffed for a fourth time when the results of the veterans committee were announced on December 7, 2009. "I don't care about legacies, I don't need validation, I know what I did."

Miller may know he turned the players association into a powerhouse, but he still has a thing or two to learn about pension law, according to Ronald Dean, an attorney based in Pacific Palisades, California who is a fellow of the College of Labor and Employment Lawyers and a charter fellow of the American College of Employee Benefits Counsel. "Under ERISA it is perfectly permissible to make an amendment retroactive even if it then vests those who were previously unvested," said Dean.[137]

Named by the *National Law Journal* as one of the top forty benefits lawyers in the country, Mr. Dean was trial and appellate counsel in 15 published Ninth Circuit Court of Appeals opinions involving ERISA issues. In the class action suit, it was the Court of Appeals for the Ninth U.S. Circuit Court in California, which, on May 22, 2006, upheld Federal Judge Manuel Real's decision to award a summary judgment to MLB.

Even Manfred conceded that it could be done, but with a caveat. "The players plan can be amended only in collective bargaining," he said in answer to a question from the author.[138]

It isn't known whether the members of the alumni association's pension committee were aware that ERISA would not prove to be the huge stumbling block they thought, and that it was actually possible to amend the vesting requirements retroactively. By the last week of September 2009, Skok, Robinson, Clyde and Neibauer seemed inclined to get whatever payments they could for the ballplayers, much to the dismay of people like Baney.

---

[137] November 15, 2009 email to the author.
[138] November 19, 2009 email to the author.

"Let's shoot for the stars, that's what I've been saying all along," said Baney. "How do we know we can't be grandfathered back into the CBA if we don't try?"

Skok, in fact, would later attempt to put a positive spin on the situation by noting that, "We are exploring many different avenues to fund 'pensions' for these guys but nothing concrete has been determined.

"The life-annuity," he added, "would be the easiest to handle outside of the current pension plan."[139] While he also acknowledged that, "we have not ruled out sometime down the road getting these guys added to the Major League Players Benefit Plan," he nonetheless conceded "we have no idea if and when that would happen."[140]

To be certain they were all on the same page about the pre-1980 players' situation, in advance of their October 1 showdown with Manfred and Weiner in Manhattan, Skok, Robinson, Clyde and Neibauer conferred with Foster during one of their regular brainstorming sessions held via conference call on September 24, 2009. Told by the association's executive director that MLB officials he had spoken to thought it would cost between $3.3 million and $7.7 million to fund annual payments to the 874 players, Robinson unveiled his own proposal to disburse life annuities to the retirees based on years of service credit, according to one of the participants in the conference call. Under his plan, the annual payments totaled $5.2 million.

Broken down by years, Robinson's plan called for the following: $3,000 per year if the player had less than one year of service; $6,000 per year if the player had between one and two

---

[139] October 26, 2009 email to the author.
[140] Ibid.

years of service, $9,000 per year if the player had between two and three years of service and $12,000 per year if the player had between three and four years of service credit.

Just how did Robinson arrive at these figures? Were they based on actuarial tables? Nope. "They were strictly off the top of his head. His numbers were what he thought would be fair," explained Skok.[141]

Not only did Foster think the numbers were fair but, according to the same conference call participant, he called Robinson's proposal "a great idea. It's just what we need."

Others were less than enthused. "I imagine it could help a lot of the guys," said Moran upon learning about Robinson's plan. "But I don't get excited anymore about this stuff. Maybe when someone sends me a piece of paper to sign, I'll get excited, but not now."

"I suppose something is better than nothing," said Jim Sadowski.

Even the normally loquacious Colbern was subdued when he was informed about Robinson's proposal. "The Lord gives you what you have on this earth," he told the author in early October 2009. "If it's the only thing we get out of this, I suppose I'd take it," he added, noting that an extra $500 per month would help defray approximately three-quarters of what he now spends out of pocket on all his various prescriptions.

"Whatever happens happens for a reason," continued Colbern. "We don't live in a perfect world, but annual payments would be something."

---

[141] Ibid.

True, annual payments would be something, but that something wouldn't include medical benefits. Nor would such payments feature survivor benefits to loved ones or designated beneficiaries.

Rahm Emanuel, the former United States Representative from Illinois who now serves as President Obama's Chief of Staff, is fond of saying that government is often a choice between bad and worse.[142] Compared to the status quo, that's essentially the choice MLB and the union would be asking these players to make. For, if it came down to accepting a life annuity instead of a pension that guaranteed survivor benefits, one would be hard pressed to argue that these players would be better off not receiving any monies at all.

"It's just not fair," said 84-year-old Bill Glynn, the former first baseman who smacked three homeruns in one game in 1954, when he was a member of the Cleveland Indians team that won 111 games during the regular season and represented the American League in the World Series against the New York Giants that year. "When a husband dies, a pension is supposed to take care of his wife."

Glynn, who stroked a pinch hit double in Game 3 of the '54 Series in his last at-bat in the majors,[143] admitted that not getting a pension from the game "is a little bit of a sore spot with me," but that he and his wife, Dolores, who once served as the secretary to Buzzie Bavasi, the president of the San Diego Padres, "have lived pretty conservatively over the last 50 years.

"After my playing days were over I bought a milk business, which turned out to be pretty good for us financially," he said. "But

---

[142] "An Inconvenient Truth Teller," Holly Bailey & Evan Thomas, *Newsweek*, October 19, 2009.
[143] Baseball-almanac.com.

I've always hoped someday that we'd get the pension. If I got one now, that'd be great."

"I'm sure every old fart like myself would jump at the chance to receive something after all these years," agreed Bill Edgerton, the former pitcher who spent his last year in baseball with the expansion Seattle Pilots in 1969. "If that idea turns out to be the payment they come up with, it might be better than nothing." Nonetheless, Edgerton, who is older than his wife, Kimberly, by more than two decades, thinks it's especially unfair that spouses might not be provided for.

"What's right is right and what's wrong is wrong," he said. "Why should my wife be penalized because Selig doesn't want to do the right thing?

"Bud Selig doesn't know his ass from the hole in the ground," continued Edgerton, who briefly worked in law enforcement in West Palm Beach, Florida before moving to Indiana to work at an AM General plant in South Bend. Now a resident of Foley, Alabama, Edgerton puts the blame squarely on the commissioner for not doing right by the pre-1980, non-vested players.

"The commissioner's office tiptoed around the race card when the game awarded the Negro Leaguers those monies," he said. "I'm perfectly fine giving them monies and saying that their contributions were just as important as mine were. But it stands to reason that, if my contributions were just as important as theirs, I should be getting money too. Well, then where's my money?"

"To me, it all boils down to the fact that you just can't buck big business," said Edgerton. "Baseball is a steamroller, and it's rolled right over guys like me."

However, some aren't bothered that Robinson's plan wouldn't take care of spouses. "I mentioned it to her, and she's okay with it," said Dillard of his wife's reaction to the proposal.

While Dillard and his better half, Elma, may be amenable to receiving the life annuity, it is a potential deal breaker for men like Wright and, in particular, Hutto.

"My wife and I talked about it and, frankly, we've got mixed emotions," said Wright. "On the one hand, after all these years, we think getting anything would be a major accomplishment. On the other hand, I keep asking myself if I really want to sell my soul just to get maybe $800 a month?"

Hutto was less conflicted. "I personally would be disappointed. Very disappointed, to tell you the truth," he said. "If a life annuity was actually offered to us, right now I'd probably say 'No thank you,' if you must know."

Hutto's reasons for prospectively refusing such a payment are especially poignant.

"I've got two daughters, and when I'm gone I'd like to leave them something that would come from baseball," he explained. "That way they'd know that my time in the game actually meant something. That would mean a lot to me."

CHAPTER 9

So just how much is a pension from Major League Baseball worth anyway?

Manfred's well-meaning aide, Courtney, tried his best to answer the author's question in July 2009. "Given the very unique nature of the Major League Baseball Players' Pension Plan, which contains a variable benefit feature, the question posed cannot be answered with any significant degree of accuracy. The benefit amount is a function of the participant's age when he accrued the service, the plan years in which the service is accrued, amount of service, 3 year average salary level and age at which benefits commence.

"The plan was designed to deliver a high comp player (one whose high 3-year average salary exceeds $68,212) an expected benefit of $112,221 at age 62 with 10 (or more) years of service assuming the variable benefit assets had earned 4.50% per year," continued Courtney. "Since the variable benefit assets have averaged more than 4.5% over time the benefit payable at age 62 would be above this figure."[144]

As for those ex-big leaguers who, like the pre-1980, non-vested players, didn't command huge salaries, the baseball pension plan would still be a valuable source of income. In a recent post, blogger Brandon Call wrote that, while the average NFL retiree's pension in 2005 was $14,500, "baseball's average pension payout in 2006 was a little more than $34,000 per player. To give further evidence of this discrepancy, a 10-year veteran of Major League Baseball will get an annual payout of $175,000. The same 10-year veteran from the NFL will be looking at $32,000."[145]

Even graduate students acknowledge the merits of the MLB pension plan. For a finance class he and three other classmates took two years ago, while attending the University of Illinois at Urbana-Champaign, Ted Nocella, who now works in the Oak Brook, Illinois offices of the prestigious accounting firm of Crowe Horwath, wrote that "the pension plan provides very good income for those players who were not superstars.

"Today, an early retirement player can even receive $85,000 annually," explained Nocella. "The retirement age is 62 for anyone who retired after 1970 and 65 for anyone who retired before then."

In their assessment of the MLB pension plan, Nocella and his fellow classmates were especially impressed by its health and welfare aspects. "The health benefit plan covers all expenses related to hospital stays for 100% of costs," according to their research paper. "Hospital stays are limited in coverage to 120 days in a semi-private room. If the beneficiary elects for a private room, the

---

[144] July 10, 2009 email to the author.
[145] Brandon Call, "No Money in Retirement," *The Bleacher Report Blog*, July 23, 2008.

plan will cover the cost of a semi-private room plus $20. Examples of services included prescription drugs, nursing costs, machine usage, and laboratory processing."

"For outpatient procedures... charges between $500 and $5,000 for an individual or $15,000 for a family of four are covered with an 80/20 co-payment by the plan," the paper continued. "Charges above the threshold are covered 100% by the plan. All major services like x-rays and surgeries are covered in full under the plan.

"In conjunction with Medicare, the plan allows election for optional supplemental comprehensive benefits," the student paper explained. "These benefits will be used for coverage beyond Medicare limitations. This is done by recalculating the benefit as if the supplement was the primary plan, and adjusting benefits to compensate for any shortfall. The supplemental coverage is similar to the general plan, with the 100% coverage thresholds raised to $10,000 and $30,000 for an individual and a family of four respectively."

Nocella and his co-authors even took time to review the dental and vision coverage offered by the league's benefit plan. "The plan provides coverage for 100% of all routine maintenance," they noted. "Coverage for major services such as root canals and orthodontics are covered in the amount of 80%. All charges in one year are limited to $5,000 in total. The vision plan covers expenses up to $75 for glass frames and $50 for glasses, with $100 per individual for contact lenses. All charges below $75 for optometrist services are covered in full."

To hammer home the practical value of collecting an MLB pension, Nocella et al even cited a *San Francisco Chronicle* article chronicling the story of Mike Norris, the former Oakland A's pitcher who had spinal-cord surgery in January 2000. Though health insurance from his nine-year baseball career covered the medical expenses, Norris' dangerous and expensive operation also required him to undergo years of physical therapy.[146]

Norris, who began collecting his major-league pension early, at age 45, receives $84,000 annually. "I'd be lost without it," he said.[147]

Sadly, most people in this country don't have any pension plan to fall back on. Citing statistics furnished by the Center for Retirement Research at Boston College, *Time* recently reported that just 21 percent of all workers in the United States today are covered by traditional pensions.[148] That's why, if anything constructive came out of the market crash of 2008, it's that Americans were forced to examine whether they are truly ready for retirement.

In a survey of 1,000 individuals conducted on behalf of the Employee Benefit Research Institute (EBRI) by Mathew Greenwald & Associates, workers who said they were confident about having enough money for a comfortable retirement hit the lowest level (13 percent) since EBRI started polling people in 1993. In addition, the results of the annual Retirement Confidence Survey (RCS) also found that the poor economy (36 percent) and the need to make up for losses in the stock market (28 percent) were the most often cited reasons for postponing retirement.[149]

Perhaps just as important, the RCS also revealed that workers who say they are very confident in having enough money to take care

[146] Ron Kroichick, "Pension in Pro Sports; An Age-Old Issue for all the Big Leagues," *San Francisco Chronicle*, March 18, 2007.
[147] Ibid.
[148] Allan Sloan, "What's Still Wrong With Wall Street," *Time*, October 19, 2009.
[149] 2009 Retirement Confidence Survey, Employee Benefit Research Institute, Issue Brief #328, April 2009.

of basic expenses in retirement dropped to 25 percent in 2009, down from 40 percent in 2007, while only 13 percent feel very confident about having enough to pay for medical expenses, which is down from 20 percent in 2007 also.[150] Among retirees, only a quarter (25 percent, down from 41 percent in 2007) of those surveyed feel very confident about covering their health expenses.[151]

And, according to the findings of a Pew Research study, 78 percent of workers over 50 now believe they will have to save substantially more as a result of the losses caused by the 2008 crash.[152]

How concerned is the American public that the economic downturn has personally hurt them over the last 18 months? According to the results of a telephone poll conducted by Abt SRBI Public Affairs over a two day period, from October 26 thru October 27, 2009, 44 percent of the 1,003 contacted feel they've been hurt some, while 23 percent report they've been hurt a great deal.[153]

Equally significant is that fact that more than one-third (36 percent) of those 1,003 people actually feel their own financial situation has gotten *worse* over the past 12 months.[154]

As a result of the downturn, the gerontology research and consulting group Age Wave reports that most people believe their retirement will need to be postponed an average of 3.6 years.[155] But baseball players aren't most people, especially since their life expectancy has actually been found to be *higher* than that of not only the general population, but that of players from the three other major league sports, as well.

---

[150] Ibid.

[151] Ibid.

[152] Brad Reagan, Elizabeth O'Brien, Daren Fonda and Reshma Kapadia, "Refresh Your Financial Life," *Smart Money*, December 2009.

[153] Allan Sloan, "Why Main Street Hates Wall Street," *Time*, November 9, 2009.

[154] Ibid.

[155] Kristen Bellstrom, "Put Off Retirement? No Way!" *Smart Money*, November 2009.

Compared to the average 20-year-old U.S. male, a MLB player can expect almost five additional years of life, according to the results of a research study published in *Social Sciences Quarterly*.[156] The study found that career length is inversely associated with the risk of death, likely because those who play longer gain additional incomes, physical fitness and training.[157]

However, as Tom Hanks' character, "Paul Edgecombe," discovered in Stephen King's *The Green Mile*, living longer isn't always a good thing. That's especially true for all those pre-1980, non-vested players who still need to work, if only because of the lousy economy.

---

[156] Jarron M. Saint Onge, Richard G. Rogers and Patrick M. Krueger, "Major League Baseball Players' Life Expectancies," *Social Sciences Quarterly*, Volume 89, Issue 3, The Southwestern Social Science Association, July 17, 2008.

[157] Ibid.

CHAPTER 10

On the day of their meeting with Manfred and Weiner, Neibauer, Eddie Robinson, Clyde, Skok, Foster and Jim Hannan, the former Brewers, Tigers and Washington Senators hurler who is chairman of the board of the alumni association, held one last strategy session during an early afternoon lunch at their hotel.

Given his title, Hannan, who pitched in 276 games and compiled a won-lost mark of 41-48 with a 3.88 ERA over 10 seasons, including a career best 10-6 record in 1968 when he played for the Senators, had been invited to take the meeting as a courtesy.[158] A onetime player representative himself, Hannan's biography on the association's website claims that it was his own master's thesis on the Major League pension plan which Miller used to acquaint himself with baseball's benefit system.

Though he may have been familiar with the pension plan, Hannan wasn't particularly trusted by the four members of his

---

[158] Baseball-almanac.com.

own pension committee. "He's wishy-washy," said one of them. "He's got the spine of a piece of spaghetti."

Agreed that no one member of the alumni group would run the meeting and do all of the talking, the four committee members, as well as Foster and Hannan, walked to the MLB offices on Park Avenue in Manhattan following lunch. Neibauer said he felt so pumped up that he told Robinson it reminded him of the adrenaline rush he used to get while warming up in the bullpen.

Joining the six-member alumni contingent at the commissioner's offices were Weiner, Rogers, Manfred and Daniel Halem, the senior vice president and general counsel for labor for MLB. Neither Selig nor Fehr were present.

Not surprisingly, one of the first topics of conversation that was discussed was the class-action lawsuit. According to one of the former players who attended the meeting, though Manfred acknowledged that his experiences dealing with Acho had been less than pleasant, "he said he wasn't going to hold that against the inactive, non-vested former players.

"Basically, he said that 'the lawsuit was water under the bridge,'" continued the player, who did not want to be identified discussing the private conversation. "And he told us, 'We (the league) want to get this done.'"

Afterwards, when asked why, after nearly three decades, MLB was now entertaining these players' situation when it didn't legally have to, Manfred responded, "We have continued this dialogue because Commissioner Selig recognizes that these players made a contribution to the game."[159]

---

[159] November 19, 2009 email to the author.

As for Weiner, the same player said the new union executive director also expressed an interest in helping the pre-1980, non-vested players. "And what he said was that he was in favor of doing a non-qualified pension plan."

Seven weeks later, on November 19, 2009, the author asked Gregory Bouris, the MLBPA communications director, just what Weiner meant when he told the alumni association members that he was in favor of a non-qualified pension plan. "I don't know how Michael characterized it," he replied. Bouris added he couldn't comment about the language Weiner had used because he personally hadn't attended the meeting.

According to a number of tax professionals, qualified retirement plans are those certified by the Internal Revenue Code Section 401(a) and ERISA. Such plans permit employers to subtract yearly permissible contributions for every participating employee, and earnings on these contributions are tax-deferred until taken out for every participant.

However, these same tax experts explained that non-qualified plans do not feature the tax benefits that qualified retirement plans offer, and do not have to be certified by either the Internal Revenue Code Section 401(a) or ERISA. Benefits, they continued, are typically paid in the form of life annuities.

Ironically, Robinson's own annuity payment proposal was not even brought up at the meeting, according to Skok. "In fact, no figures were mentioned at all," he said. "Both these guys (Manfred and Weiner) seemed very interested in getting something done, but no particulars were discussed in this meeting."[160]

---

[160] October 26, 2009 email to the author.

Both Clyde and Neibauer indicated they wanted to broach one other item with Manfred and Weiner at the meeting, but didn't. In separate interviews, each man contended it would be possible to help fund payments to the pre-1980, non-vested players just from the monies generated by products licensed by MLB. "Whatever we wind up getting, you could fund the whole damn thing just from the licensing agreements alone," said Neibauer.

Examples of such products include trading cards, video games, tee-shirts, caps, pennants, posters, pins and action figures. All players receive a pro-rated share of licensing revenue that is determined by their actual days of major league service in a given season.[161]

In 2007 alone, sales of team caps and tee-shirts reportedly totaled more than $3.3 billion. Another $505 million was made from corporate sponsorships, such as the one MLB has enjoyed for more than nine decades with Gillette. And television rights brought in an additional $670 million.[162]

Besides the conditions established by MLB Properties—the licensor—to be a prospective licensee of Major League Baseball, "any company seeking to use the names or likenesses of more than two Major League Baseball players in connection with a commercial product, product line or promotion must sign a licensing agreement with the MLBPA. The license grants the use of the players' names and/or likenesses only and not the use of any MLB team logos or marks."[163]

[161] Major League Baseball Players Association website.
[162] Chris Cotter, "America's Greatest Business Rivals: NFL Tries To Tackle MLB," *Fox Business*, July 13, 2009.
[163] Major League Baseball Players Association website.

What *was* discussed was the correspondence that Foster said Manfred and Weiner had agreed to write, according to the same player who attended the meeting. At some point, he continued, somebody reminded Manfred and Weiner about their promise to write the letter, and they both reiterated their commitment to doing so.

After some more discussion, the two-hour meeting finally came to an end. But not before Robinson got in a dig at Rogers as both men were leaving the commissioner's offices, according to an eyewitness to the exchange.

"I don't get it, Steve," the elder statesman of the alumni association group told the special assistant to the executive director of the players association. "I don't get *you*. Why won't you help these guys out? You played with many of them, didn't you? Morally, you guys know you're completely wrong on this, don't you?"

Robinson later described the October 1, 2009 summit as "a success."[164] So did Clyde, who called the meeting between the parties "historic. To the best of my knowledge, I believe it was the first time all the principals got together in the same room to discuss this issue face-to-face."

As promised, Manfred and Weiner sent the following email to Foster three weeks later, on October 22, 2009:

> On behalf of both the Office of the Commissioner and the Major League Baseball Players Association, we appreciate the efforts of the Alumni Association in initiating a constructive dialogue regarding the group of inactive players who did not satisfy the four-year vesting

[164] Personal note to the author.

requirement of the players' pension plan in effect when they played. Both the Commissioner's Office and the Players Association recognize the important contributions to the game made by former players, and take seriously the concerns raised by the Alumni Association. We found the recent meeting in New York on this subject to be quite helpful.

At that meeting, the Commissioner's Office explained that this question can only be addressed meaningfully as part of the collective bargaining negotiations with the Association. During the 2006 round of bargaining, the Union included the subject of inactive, non-vested players in its package of proposals regarding the Benefit Plan. Against the backdrop of the litigation commenced against the Commissioner's Office by certain former non-vested players, the proposal was not well received. Due to the efforts of the Alumni Association led by Dan Foster and Eddie Robinson, the ill-will created by that litigation has greatly dissipated.

The next round of bargaining is expected to commence in 2011. At the meeting, the Union explained that the status of non-vested players again will be in the mix of Benefit Plan issues the active players will consider in formulating bargaining proposals. The Commissioner's Office, in turn, stated that, although it has no legal obligation to negotiate with the Union over non-vested players, it is willing to discuss this important issue at the bargaining table.

The bargaining parties made clear at the meeting that no one can predict or commit as to what agreement negotiations in 2011 might produce. Preliminarily, we made plain that all 2011 bargaining matters had to be discussed with our respective constituents, a process that was only in its initial stages. We explained that many other Benefit Plan issues would also be considered for bargaining in 2011, including many of great concern to Alumni Association members—funding of benefits for current retirees, potential benefit improvements for inactive vested members, potential inclusion of additional coaches as Plan participants, among others. All present also recognized that the downturn and continued uncertainty in the financial markets will make for a challenging environment for the next Benefit Plan negotiations.

Again, we thank all of the representatives of the Alumni Association who attended the recent meeting in New York. You communicated clearly and effectively your passion for this issue and your sincere concern for the human consequences for these players and their families. While no promises can be made as to the ultimate outcome, you can be certain that the status of non-vested players will be given serious consideration in the context of the 2011 collective bargaining negotiations. We look forward to continuing to work with you and the Alumni Association in the future.

The Manfred and Weiner email was sent to all the 874 ballplayers as an enclosure with the Raise the Bar letter, which was at long last sent after having been shelved for more than two months. Dated October 30, 2009, the letter, which was signed by Skok, started making its way into the mailboxes of the ex-players in early November.

Predictably, reactions to the Manfred and Weiner communication ran the gamut.

"This committee has apparently done us some good," said Dillard upon receiving the pair of letters. "But it sounds like nothing much will be done until 2011, if they do anything at all."

"I was disappointed by the letter, but I really wasn't expecting anything different," said Baney. "I mean, nobody committed to anything except more discussion. It was all pretty bland."

Upon viewing the email for the first time, the author himself wondered what, if anything, both Manfred and Weiner had actually committed themselves to? As Manfred himself had told Foster at the All-Star Game in July, there was no way that a new CBA could be written which included amending the vesting requirements for the pre-1980 players. If there really was no way to write these players into the next CBA, then why would MLB's Executive Vice-President for Labor Relations and Human Resources indicate he would try to do so in December 2011, when the current CBA is up?

"The premise of your question is incorrect," replied Manfred when asked this very question by the author. "What we told the group in the meeting in October was that the most likely place to get the kind of joint solution favored by the Commissioner was in the process of collective bargaining. We committed to have the issue on the table, we did not commit to a particular outcome. The solution to this issue could take many forms and I am not prepared to comment further."[165]

Clyde was perhaps the most disappointed by the tone of the Manfred/Weiner email. "They're talking about maybe doing something in the next CBA? Listen, our item would be the first that gets thrown out of those negotiations if the economy keeps tanking," he said. "It doesn't take a village idiot to figure that out."

As for the players association, though both Weiner and Rogers were asked to comment on the record, neither man ever responded to the author's repeated requests for an interview. Instead, on November 19, 2009, Bouris issued a prepared statement that he read to the author. "The Major League Baseball Players Association looks forward to continuing what has been a constructive dialogue on this subject with both MLB and the Alumni Association."

The détente was short-lived. Less than two weeks later, on November 30, 2009, nobody from the Alumni Association was permitted to address the executive board of the players union at their annual meeting in Scottsdale, Arizona.

---

[165] November 19, 2009 email to the author.

Home

CHAPTER 11

Though their treatment of the pre-1980, non-vested players has left a foul taste in the mouths of many—Acho, for example, said that, though he used to idolize Brooks Robinson *the player* while growing up, he no longer holds Brooks Robinson *the man* in the same high esteem—it would be wrong to assume that both the league and the players association are heartless, cold and unfeeling entities.

For example, in 1999, MLB and the MLBPA teamed up to establish a grant program—the Baseball Tomorrow Fund (BTF)—to support youth sports. In 2009 alone, the fund awarded some $2.6 million to nearly 70 youth organizations.

In concert with the McCormick Foundation, the league last year also launched an initiative, Welcome Back Veterans, designed to raise $100 million for mental-health clinics and help returning servicemen find jobs and job training.

Like Merritt, Nellie King is a veteran of the armed forces who proudly served this country during the Korean War. Not much bothers the 81-year-old King, who takes in stride the fact that he was diagnosed with Parkinson's two years ago. He has even come to accept the fact that he now lives at Friendship Village, a retirement home in Upper St. Clair, Pennsylvania, while his wife of 56 years, Bernadette, is confined to the Devonshire of Mount Lebanon Assisted Living Center, in Pittsburgh.

Signed as an amateur free agent in 1946, King didn't make his major league debut until 1954. Three years later, at the age of 29, he was out of baseball because of the "dead arm" he says he developed. He subsequently worked a variety of odd jobs he despised just to make ends meet, including caddying at a golf course and being behind the cash register at a liquor store.

Years later, after he had cemented his professional reputation as a great storyteller who, along with the late Bob Prince, routinely entertained listeners with his calls of Pittsburgh Pirate games on the radio, King endured the public humiliation of being fired by Westinghouse Broadcasting in 1975. And, more recently, when money was tight, he swallowed his pride and sought financial assistance from BAT, just like Colbern did.

Now in the twilight of his life, King remains hopeful that one day, maybe sometime soon, he and all the rest of the pre-1980, non-vested ballplayers will indeed start to receive pensions from MLB. "I sure could use it, I won't deny it," he told a caller recently.

Through much of the last six decades, King has remained cheery and even-keeled because he says he took to heart some advice proffered to him and other Pirate minor leaguers by none other than Branch Rickey. Rickey, of course, was the executive vice-president and general manager of the Pirates who had helped integrate baseball in 1947 when he famously signed Jackie Robinson to a contract while serving as president of the Brooklyn Dodgers.

"Mr. Rickey was fond of telling us this story about a commercial painter who kept being distracted from his job by this stray dog," recalled King. "He would say, 'All the painter wanted to do was pet the dog, but it kept running away from him. Finally, when he returned in earnest to his work, when he wasn't looking, that's when he felt the dog cozy up by his leg.'

"It was Rickey's own parable for a road map to success in life," explained King. "He would tell us, 'Boys, you can't get up in the morning and say you're going to be happy today, because you can't will happiness to occur. Just like that painter who always tried to reach and grab at that dog. The more he attempted to pet the dog, the more it ran away from him. Same thing applies to life. The more you try to get something, the more you fail. When you're not trying, you usually get what you want. When you least expect it, happiness will embrace you.' "

Rickey's advice left such an impression on King that he based the title of his autobiographical memoir, *Happiness Is Like A Cur Dog: The Thirty-Year Journey of a Major League Baseball Pitcher and Broadcaster* (Author House), on that one story.

While that story's lesson is certainly instructive, and most people would be well-served to heed it, the inactive, pre-1980, non-vested players would be wise not to. That's because neither the league nor the union have given them any reason to believe anything to the contrary. As Clyde himself noted, the players have "been relying on the owners' sense of fairness for nearly 30 years."

Nonetheless, the October 1, 2009 face-to-face meeting in Manhattan was important if only because there was a frank exchange of views and positions by both sides. And, if Manfred and Weiner are to be taken at their word, then the October 22, 2009 letter they jointly penned should be viewed favorably by the players. Whether it results in a breakthrough in this long-standing impasse is anybody's guess but, for now, there is not as much distrust in the air.

However, if both the league and the union are genuinely and sincerely committed actually to want to help these players, they shouldn't have to wait until the next CBA negotiations begin. Though the learned rabbi and therapist Abraham J. Twerski once observed, "Putting things off is so common that it can hardly be considered abnormal behavior,"[166] with the economy in a downward spiral, those pre-1980, non-vested ballplayers can't afford to wait much longer for this matter to be attended to.

When trying to resolve a dispute, it is often difficult to gauge whether tangible progress has been made. After three decades, this ongoing matter is no different. But perhaps that October 1, 2009 meeting and the follow-up correspondence from Manfred and Weiner portend better things to come.

"We don't see the end of the tunnel," said the late President John F. Kennedy during a press conference he held on December 12, 1962, "but I don't think it is darker than it was a year ago, and in some ways, it is lighter."[167] That was how the 35th President of the United States responded to a reporter's question about U.S. troop strength in Vietnam, and whether he intended to scale back our military presence there.

---

[166] Abraham J. Twerski, M.D., *When Do the Good Things Start?* Topper Books, 1988, p. 89.
[167] John F. Kennedy Presidential Library & Museum, National Archives and Records Administration, Press Conferences of President Kennedy, News Conference 46.

Forty-eight years later, that same response could probably sum up the situation faced by the pre-1980, non-vested players.

Photo Gallery

Steve Grilli, circa 1976, when he was a member of the Detroit Tigers. Grilli, who pitched in a total of 70 games over parts of four seasons with the Tigers, says he has nothing to show for his time in the big leagues. "I feel like I'm just being swept under the carpet," he says.

Ron Kittle, who was the American League Rookie of the Year in 1983, is now a motivational speaker whose nonprofit foundation, Indiana Sports Charities, is dedicated to eradicating cancer. "If they deserve it," he said of the pre-1980, non-vested players' efforts to be awarded pensions, "they should get it."

Darcy Fast, when he was a pitcher for the Chicago Cubs in 1968.

Darcy Fast, the senior pastor at the Centralia Community Church of God in Centralia, Washington.

Gary Neibauer, when he was a member of the Atlanta Braves. Neibauer, who hurled a hitless inning of relief against the Mets in the 1969 National League Championship Series, is on the special Major League Baseball Players Alumni Association committee, attempting to have pensions awarded to the remaining pre-1980, non-vested players.

Gary Neibauer and his wife, Christine, circa 2009.

David Clyde, circa 2009. The former number-1 overall choice in the 1973 draft, Clyde was just 37 days shy of meeting the four-year vesting requirement for a pension.

Craig Skok, circa 1973, when he debuted as a pitcher for the Boston Red Sox. Years later, when he missed the four-years vesting requirement by only two weeks, Skok telephoned former Atlanta Braves owner Ted Turner to ask to be called up to the team in order to qualify for a pension.

Eddie Robinson, the four-time All-Star and former general manager, says that Hall of Famer Early Wynn's actions to increase pensions in 1990 inspired him to help the pre-1980, non-vested players.

The three Sadowski brothers, from left, Ted, Bob & Ed,
in happier times. Ted and Ed died within five months of
one another, in 1993. Their nephew, Jim Sadowski, says he
is "obsessed" with getting Bob, the only one of the three
brothers who is still alive, a pension.

Don Dillard, circa 1961, when he was a pinch hitter extraordinaire for the Cleveland Indians.

Don Dillard today. Injured on a freak play in a game against the Dodgers, Dillard's double vision affects him the most whenever he walks into a movie theatre and has to adjust his eyes to the dark.

Ernie Fazio, the first player ever signed by the expansion Houston Colt .45s, was one of the lead plaintiffs in the class-action suit filed against Major League Baseball in 2003. Fazio, who has spent the better part of the last three decades working in the refuse business, believes he and all the other pre-1980, non-vested players are now part of baseball's garbage heap.

Dick Baney, when he was a member of the expansion Seattle Pilots, in 1969. Angered that he isn't receiving a pension, Baney wanted to "embarrass" baseball by mounting a protest at the 2009 All-Star Game in St. Louis.

Dick Baney in 2009.

Rick Grottanelli, at left, and Harry "The Horse" Danning, shortly after being informed that all the pre-1947 players would receive annual $10,000 payments from Major League Baseball, in 1997. The pair's closeness and respect for one another was so great that, upon learning that Danning had lost the championship ring he had earned in 1933 as a member of the New York Giants, Grottanelli called up the company that made the ring and paid to have a replacement issued to his friend.

"Sports do not build character. They reveal it."

– Heywood Campbell Broun
Founder, American Newspaper Guild
(December 7, 1888 – December 18, 1939)

WA